Careers in the Travel Industry

Careers in the Travel Industry

FOURTH EDITION

**CAROLE CHESTER AND
VERITÉ REILY COLLINS**

KOGAN PAGE
CAREERS
SERIES

First published in 1985
Second edition 1989
By Carole Chester, entitled *Careers in the Holiday Industry*
Third edition 1992
By Carole Chester and Christine Swanson,
entitled *Careers in the Travel Industry*
Fourth edition 1994
By Carole Chester and Verité Reily Collins

Kogan Page Limited
120 Pentonville Road
London N1 9JN

© Kogan Page Limited 1985, 1989, 1992, 1994

British Library Cataloguing in Publication Data

A CIP record for this book is available from the British Library.

ISBN 0-7494-1271-2

Typeset by Books Unlimited (Nottm), Sutton-in-Ashfield, NG17 1AL
Printed and bound in Great Britain by Clays Ltd, St Ives plc

Contents

Introduction

By the year 2000 it is expected that tourism will be the world's biggest employer, offering jobs ranging from IT (information technology), the hospitality industry (hotels, restaurants, self-catering etc) and transport, to looking after people as representatives, receptionists and guides.

Although entrants into the industry are generally poorly paid even after training (see advertisements), once you have gained experience, salaries compare favourably with other industries.

Travel is regarded as an essential part of the job and it is said that working in tourism gives you a chance to live like a millionaire on a basic salary. If you want a 9 to 5 job then the large tour operators need office staff in administration and telephone sales. Marketing and contracting, however, can entail working long hours, and anyone whose job brings them into contact with the public knows that if there is a crisis, their day can last over 24 hours with no time off in lieu.

On the plus side you are often thanked by clients for having just done your job!

Languages are very useful, but conversely it is said that 80 per cent of the world's tourism is 'handled' in English.

Like all industries, the travel industry has its ups and downs and in this book we will try to give you an idea of both.

Are You Suited to Travel?

There are so many aspects to travel that almost anyone can be suited to a career in this field. It is more a question of being able to pick your way through the myriad choices. Those with creative flair might look to marketing, promotion, public relations, journalism or photography, whereas those who can enthuse about someone else's idea or product may find their *métier* is sales. Individuals who prefer detailed organisational work will find that a grounding in finance or computers will stand them in good stead. But if your skills involve dealing with people, the service sector has plenty of scope.

Just think – an airline pilot or stewardess working in the travel industry, and a hairdresser or waiter on board a passenger liner, are both considered to be in travel-related professions. These days, hotel managers often shift from hotel to hotel around the world and chefs are constantly lecturing and visiting abroad.

If you have a disability then you have to be selective: ie, dyslexics often make excellent guides and NVQs (National Vocational Qualifications) with work-based assessment mean there are no written exams.

If you are in a wheelchair then generally insurance companies will not allow you to work on a coach or in an airliner. But there are so many jobs that will suit, and most tourist venues, hotels and other places to work have good wheelchair access. Most local tourist boards can advise you on member companies that might have jobs.

What Skills?

It would be far too difficult to say that you need a specific skill to obtain a specific job in travel. A lot of training is given once you have been employed. On the other hand, you could hardly expect to become a chef if you cannot boil an egg, or a rep or tour guide if you hate the sight of people. If you thought serving others was beneath you, a ship's steward or cabin crew position is not for you.

Assess your own skills before you choose a career. Talk to your college careers office, your family and friends. Pay attention to your own presentation, be it the letters you write or your appearance. Be prepared to take a lowly post initially and work your way up from within. The best degree in the world is not going to make you a manager overnight.

What Courses?

What courses are best for you depends primarily on which aspect of travel you intend to tackle. To help simplify matters, think of the tourism industry as three major sectors: accommodation and catering; travel and transport; leisure, recreation and entertainment.

The greatest number of job opportunities lie in the first of these sectors. Courses to consider would therefore concentrate on hotel and catering management; sales and marketing; administration, business and accounting skills. Management and marketing qualifications would also be useful in the recreational or leisure areas and the travel and transport fields, though the latter is not expanding quite so fast. There are limited opportunities with local authorities and government agencies in the tourism area, but applicants will be expected to be thoroughly knowledgeable about the product or area they are to promote, for anything but the most junior positions. Travel and tourism as a degree course subject is relatively new, but the courses on offer are increasing yearly and are available at colleges and universities all over the UK and Europe. With membership of the European Community students have the option of taking a course in another country, particularly if there is a language requirement. Switzerland is well known for its excellent hotel schools, and the Central Bureau for Educational Visits particularly recommends the Ecole Hôtelier de Lausanne; the Swiss National Tourist Office can give details of other courses recognised world-wide.

GNVQ (General National Vocational Qualifications)
There is one for Leisure and Tourism, but as far as is known the tourism industry did not have any input into the original specifications, and tour operators may not accept GNVQs as a qualification. If your school or college offers GNVQs, ask if the teachers have any industry qualification or have worked in the industry.

ABTA says it is better to do a level 1 NVQ (SVQ in Scotland), but if you have to do GNVQs, *insist* on doing the optional paper on Travel Geography, which is the only section that has universal industry approval.

YT Courses
ABTA runs these for trainees aged 16 to 18 wanting a career working in travel agencies. They recommend that you find a local travel agent prepared to take you on for training. This is difficult, but you may find one by asking around, or contacting

agencies that advertise in *Yellow Pages* and in travel ads in local newspapers.

If you cannot find an agent to take you on, contact ABTA who will put your CV on their database to match up with any travel agent who might want a trainee in your area.

Choosing a Training Course or College

Once you have decided what training you need, how do you choose the college or training establishment that suits *you*?

How Do I Find The Most Suitable Course?
1. Ask someone working in the industry
2. Ask employers what qualifications are needed and if they can recommend a course or college
3. Send a large sae to the appropriate association or authority (addresses in Chapter 12).

How Do I Choose A College Or Training Establishment?
1. How are you treated when you telephone?
2. Are you kept waiting for anyone to answer the phone?
3. Does the switchboard handle your enquiry courteously and put you through to the right extension?
4. Once through, is the person helpful or does he or she just try to send out leaflets which may not answer your enquiries?
5. If you ask for leaflets, do they arrive within a week?

Incidentally, if you are asked to send an sae that probably means the course is well known and they receive more enquiries than places – so it's good!

How your enquiry is handled can tell you a lot about a college and its efficiency. Apathy towards teaching standards spreads throughout, and if support staff such as telephonists can't do their job properly, imagine what the teaching will be like.

Incidentally, when I asked for information from the Lausanne Hotel School in Switzerland my fax was answered by another fax with all the information – within the hour! No wonder people in the industry told me time after time that this was the best school. I am still waiting for some information from British colleges!

When You Visit the College or Training Establishment:
1. Ask who are lecturers/ teachers
   What experience have they had in the industry?

(NVQ requirements say they must have up-to-date experience and one of the reasons GNVQs may not be accepted by an employer is that the test specifications were written by academics who weren't up to date with EC laws.)
2. Ask if the college has an open day/evening where you can meet teachers
3. What are the safety standards? Are fire exits marked clearly and free of obstructions?
4. Would you like to use the loos?

If the college doesn't care about 3 and 4, or you think has unacceptable standards – high standards are so important in tourism – ask yourself, is the college capable of providing the right training?

What Qualifications?

The industry is in the process of developing NVQs (National Vocational Qualifications – SVQs in Scotland) but this takes time; that is why it is essential to ask companies what qualifications they are currently looking for. Awarding bodies can also tell you what NVQs are available or suggest suitable alternatives (see Chapter 12 for addresses).

You can work for NVQs part-time or full-time in a college or other approved organisation (see Chapter 12 for a list of addresses). If you are already employed in the industry, you can obtain an NVQ while working.

NVQs are on five levels:

Level 1 Operative level; simple tasks
Level 2 Operative level; more complex tasks, some responsibility
Level 3 Supervisory
Level 4 Management
Level 5 Senior Management

Here is a sample of NVQs (SVQs in Scotland) already available for Catering and Hospitality:

Level 1
Catering and Hospitality
 • Food Preparation and Cooking – General
 • Food Preparation and Cooking – Quick Service

- Serving Food and Drink – Bar
- Serving Food and Drink – Counter
- Serving Food and Drink – Table/Tray
- Housekeeping
- Reception and Portering
- Guest Service

Level 2
Catering and Hospitality
- Food Preparation and Cooking
- Serving Food and Drink – Restaurant
- Serving Food and Drink – Bar
- Reception
- General

Level 3
Catering and Hospitality Supervisory Management
- Food Preparation and Cooking
- Food and Drink Service
  (3 routes: table, counter, drinks)
- Housekeeping
- Reception
  (3 routes: general, functions, portering)

On-Licensed Premises Supervisory Management

Level 4
Catering and Hospitality Management
- Food Preparation and Cooking
- Food and Drink Service (2 routes: food, drinks)
- Housekeeping
- Reception (2 routes: general, functions)

On-Licensed Premises Management

Awarding Bodies
BTEC (Business and Technology Education Council)
City and Guilds of London Institute
Hotel and Catering Training Company
Royal Society of Arts
University of Oxford Delegacy of Local Examinations

What Salaries?

Anything from £5,000 pa to £50,000 plus can be offered, according to the job. To give you some idea, the following advertisements were taken from 1993 trade publications.

Some references might need an explanation. *Galileo* is a computer program. *FIT* means fully inclusive tour. *COTAC* is currently being superseded by other qualifications, and is described below. It is the Certificate of Travel Agency Competence which at level 1 also leads to the Certificate in Travel Skills, or at level 2 to the Diploma in Travel Skills, and is widely accepted throughout the trade. Generally, it would take around 18 months to get to level 1 of COTAC, and would normally involve some attendance at a college.

INCOMING TOUR OPERATIONS London   c£10-12,000++

Inbound tours experience required – planning, costing and operating UK tours for special interest groups – fluent German and/or other European language required for various positions.

BUSINESS TRAVEL/MARINE   City   to £16,000

Five years' min experience in business or ships crew travel, with fares and ticketing to Level III required for busy, expanding department. Galileo/PAMS proficiency also essential.

BRANCH MANAGER
c£10,000 + Bonus + Commission
Minimum 5 years' ABTA experience and COTAC II

ASSISTANT MANAGER
c£8,600 + Bonus + Commission
Minimum 4 years' ABTA experience and COTAC II

LONG HAUL SUPERVISOR
c£8,000 + Commission
COTAC II required

TRAVEL ADVISERS
Full time or Part time Birmingham Airport
c£7,500 + Commission
COTAC I essential

JUNIOR TRAVEL CLERKS
from £5,250 + Commission
COTAC I preferred

Experience is vital, but we also look for people with the personality and flair to gain our customers' confidence, and the initiative to make a real impact on our businesses.

In return you'll receive all the benefits you'd expect from a market leading company, and the security of being part of one of the Midlands' leading businesses.

To apply, please send your full CV indicating which vacancy and location you are applying for, to:

RESERVATIONS MANAGER
NORTH WEST
Salary c£15,000

Our client, part of a major PLC, is a profitable specialist tour operator. Due to expansion they now require immediately a RESERVATIONS MANAGER.

You should have previous experience in a supervisory role preferably with a tour operator and have the skills to motivate a team of seven staff. In addition, you will be able to manage the inventory for hotel beds and aircraft seats.

For an initial discussion please call or write with a full CV.

FRANCE

Chalet girls required for the Alps to work the 1993/94 winter ski season. Only qualified cooks will be accepted with preference given to French speakers. If interested please contact

---

This is your opportunity to join the Midlands' leading travel group – an organisation that has over 45 successful agencies across the region. We can offer individual responsibility and good prospects.

TRAVEL CONSULTANTS
c£7,500 – £8,300 + Commission
Minimum 3 years' ABTA experience. COTAC 1 essential.

SENIOR TRAVEL CLERK
(Full and part-time) c£7,000 pro rata + Commission
Minimum 3 years' ABTA experience and COTAC 1.

Experience is vital, but we also look for people with the personality and flair to gain our customers' confidence, and the initiative to make a real impact on our business. So, if you're seeking greater responsibility, this is the right company for you.

To apply, please send your full CV indicating which vacancy and location you are applying for, to

---

Travel Agency

Due to continuing expansion we require ambitious, self-motivated individuals to join this leading wholesale tour operating company. Based in our London head office, we have vacancies in our busy hotel reservations department and FIT operations department. Opportunities to progress to hotel contract negotiations and sales for the right people.

European/Middle-Eastern languages an advantage
Salary negotiable according to age and experience

Please apply in writing enclosing a full cv to:

Alternatively visit our stand at the World Travel Market

TRAVEL PERSONNEL

BUSINESS TRAVEL CONSULTANTS/MANAGERS needed with Worldspan/Galileo and BA2. Salary ranges from £12-20,000 aae.

RESERVATIONS CONSULTANT for long-haul tour operator. Must have Galileo and experience of Far East/Caribbean £13-14,000.

ADMIN MANAGER Our client needs a very efficient and competent administrator to run a department within a busy and expanding tour operation. Involves issuing itineraries, vouchers, charter tickets and all special requirements. Must be computer literate. Salary negotiable.

REGIONAL SALES EXECUTIVE for south east to develop business for established company supplying computer systems to agents. Must have proven sales track record, be self-motivating and able to cover a large area. £25-30,000 OTE.

TRAVEL COMPANY
require
Business/Consol Travel Consultant

With a minimum 2 years' retail or business house experience. We are a rapidly expanding company and you would become part of our enthusiastic professional team. Galileo training will be given.

BERMUDA

Deluxe 5-star hotel. Positions available for maitre d's, sommeliers, silver service waiters and chefs de partie. Interviews now for commencement March/April 1994. Applicants must be aged over 21 and have a minimum of 3 to 4 years' experience in 4/5-star hotels.

Chapter 1

Tour Operators

What is a Tour Operator?

A tour operator is anyone who has put together a holiday package to offer for sale. In most cases this means a company which has established respect and credibility. The company may be an independent one, one of a group of companies, or a giant holiday operation such as Kuoni, Thomson or Neckerman.

Travel agencies may also be tour operators if they create their own specialised holiday programmes, or they can be an affiliated retail element, eg Thomas Cook. Usually, though, they are straightforward retail outlets selling airline tickets and the packages of a number of operators in return for commission.

Most tour operators choose to sell their product through travel agencies because it gives them a wider coverage of the market, ie throughout the country, but some sell direct to the public with the aid of publicity and advertising. The larger companies will offer a broad range of holidays; the smaller tend to specialise in a particular destination, age group or type of vacation such as skiing.

How does a Tour Operation Work?

The aim is to offer customers something they could not obtain themselves – at least without inconvenience, effort and, more than likely, greater expenditure. By purchasing airline seat space or hotel room accommodation in bulk, the operator is given a better price than the individual and is able to pass on some of that saving. Similarly, since the operator is involved in group movements, he or she can arrange airport transfers and inexpensive insurance easily.

Costing is one of the most important features: the wholesale price of every holiday segment must be added together, plus a built-in profit. Obviously, commission payments, operation costs and overheads must be taken into consideration before a final consumer price is reached, yet that final price must appeal to the customer if the package is to sell.

Career Possibilities

The giants have many divisions of work so the choice of careers in travel and tourism is a wide one. A firm like Thomson's will have its own accountancy department, personnel office and sales reps, for example. There are contracts managers and operations managers for different areas of the world, and tour guides and reps in various destinations. A company as well known as this one will have a large management and marketing team plus its own press office and, not surprisingly, a big reservations staff.

Smaller companies operate likewise but with fewer staff and with work titles that may encompass more than one area of the business. And that goes for the specialists too, although knowledge of a specific language, sport etc will help you get to the top more quickly.

As far as the salary is concerned, for the person who builds his or her own tour operation, the sky's the limit. If you become the managing director of your own private company, you will be able to set your salary according to profits – or sell out to (or merge with) a larger holding company. Salaries in other mentioned areas are in line with those in other industries, though coach tour guides are in a bracket to themselves.

Freelance?

No way! Not as a tour operator. But many reps and tour guides are semi-freelance, since they work on a seasonal basis as part-time employees instead of full-time staff. Tour operators also need to show their product; hence a brochure must be compiled, written, illustrated and printed. This often requires freelance copywriters and travel photographers.

Becoming a Tour Operator

There are no set rules as to how to become a tour operator (as opposed to working for one). You cannot expect to become one overnight – indeed, it is generally accepted that you need a good few years in the travel industry before you could consider it – and yet an entrepreneurial person with a good idea can start a business that may eventually prove successful.

Ground Handlers

We have talked about the giants of the industry who organise tours all over the world. However, any tourist destination will have local agencies who look after incoming visitors, often on behalf of these tour operators. These agencies are incoming tour handlers, generally known as ground handlers (because they usually look after arrangements 'on the ground', and don't handle air or ferry transport).

Such companies need office staff who are good at administration and able to work on their own initiative. This can be extremely interesting as you have to visit the hotels and venues to check them out, often for a short stay at the hotel's expense, to see which are suitable for your company's clients.

Ground handlers also need interpreters, guides, tour managers, meet-and-greet staff at airports and coach drivers (see pages 21–2).

Case Studies

Churchill Family Holidays was started by two men in 1981, each with a vast amount of varied experience. Mike's background was almost all travel (a lot with Thomson's), starting as an overseas tour guide, moving into contracting and then back in the UK in the planning division and finally into sales. Between times, he worked in several travel agencies in a number of capacities. His partner, Peter, trained in marketing and finance although originally he took a degree in civil engineering.

It took them a year to obtain City financing, which they acquired by showing there was a market for their product and that they were offering something new and different; therefore, there was no competition.

> The hole in the market was that no tour operator was catering *exclusively* for families. Selling a family holiday is like selling two types of holiday simultaneously – pleasing parents and pleasing children in all their age groups.

By offering such facilities as night-time room patrols, mothers' rooms equipped with washing machines, irons etc, and three mini clubs for different age groups of children, their company has proved successful enough to attract buyers and they are now part of the Falcon Leisure Group, the umbrella name for several holiday companies.

Iris, who started Matthews Family Holidays, however, had absolutely no travel trade training. She had studied accountancy and law, subsequently very useful subjects, but at that time she was a full-time mother, bored with only doing household chores.

> It started because we bought a couple of caravans for our own holidays in France. The twins were very young so the type of holiday was ideal, and other friends with small children often stayed too.

It was the friends and relatives who suggested that the Matthews start renting out the caravans when they were not using them themselves.

> At the time, few people had seen the size of caravan we had, so they were very popular. We could have rented them several times over so, over the years, we gradually added more.

Eight years ago, the couple owned 50 caravans and Iris's husband could afford to give up his engineering job.

> We privately let them and arranged ferry services, first with Townsend Thoresen and then Brittany Ferries. Then I discovered there was such a thing as inclusive tour operators and we included ferry transportation in the package.

When the operation became too big to work from home, the Matthews wanted a shop in the village. However, the law said it had to be a travel agency and they had to pay to become members of the Association of British Travel Agents (ABTA) (see Chapter 2).

> Initially we hired a senior person, but over the years I worked in the travel shop and learnt the business myself. As soon as our International Air Transport Association (IATA) licence [see Chapter 2] came through, I took British Caledonian's air ticketing courses 1 and 2. These can only be taken once you're in the travel business.

At first, the holidays were advertised in newspapers such as *The Sunday Times* and a printed leaflet was sent in response to any enquiries. Twelve years ago, the Matthews launched their first proper brochure. Today there are 5 full-time and some 15 part-time staff (not counting those working in the agency), plus the couple themselves. And the caravans now number over 300.

Andrew took a first degree in agricultural economy and followed it up with a postgraduate course in agricultural marketing. After a couple of jobs, including several years with a regional English tourist board, he came up with a great idea for becoming a tour operator.

> Because I was working in the tourist board, I discovered there were many farmhouses in the area with rooms to let. The owners were eager for publicity but individually didn't have the financing to do it properly. What they needed was co-ordination – marketing.

That was the start of Country Farm Holidays; it took the form of a small brochure listing 40 farmhouses, all in the heart of England.

> Originally, I worked from home and it meant a lot of legwork, from assessing the properties and coaxing the owners to participate, to stuffing mailers into envelopes and taking bookings.

His good idea certainly worked. The programme now operates from an office with full-time staff, and the listed properties (which now include other self-catering units) number 350 and are to be found throughout the country.

Is Tour Operation Work for You?

Do you like people? Do your friends say you have a nice personality? Are you good at organising? Are you clever with ideas and following them through? Do you pay attention to detail? If you can say 'yes' to at least one of these questions, working for a tour operator or learning to become one might be the very career.

The travel industry as a whole, by its very character, is a people-orientated one. Enjoying personal travel is a start but concern for other people's needs and demands is the core of any travel-related job. At manager/director level, you would be expected to give interviews, speak on radio and/or appear on TV. You would, after all, be speaking for your own (or someone else's) company.

A public relations officer handling a travel account, either in-house or as part of a consultancy, has to be able to liaise with the managing director, the marketing department, sometimes an advertising agency, maybe the public, and always the press.

Those with titles in planning, contracts or operations have to liaise with airlines, hotels, car hire and other local ground operators to produce an acceptable and realistically priced end product. They must have enough knowledge to forecast how their product will expand while being profitable, or when to drop a particular programme. They must be aware of the competition and keep their ear to the ground in so far as the travelling public is concerned.

Travel reps and coach tour guides are the 'upfront' members of a tour operation – those with direct contact with the public. They may well have to work unsocial hours and be prepared to deal with unexpected problems and situations.

On the other hand, those connected with finance or reservations must pay attention to detail or thousands of holidays would not work. A pleasant telephone voice and the ability to use a computer, telex and fax are helpful in the reservations department.

Pros and Cons

Do not expect a career in tourism to be all glamour. Yes, at top level you will have travel benefits and an excellent salary, but pressure is high. Bear in mind that most of the job opportunities in a tour operation are for travel technicians or tour guides. The former is the back-room clerical variety, unlikely to be given many perks; the latter, while certainly having the chance to work abroad, does not earn a great deal for work that entails long hours, often for seven days a week.

Case Studies

Michelle worked for a large British company with tours to Corfu, Greece, for the summer season from April to October. As the operator had no winter season she returned to London to work in an office as a temporary administrative assistant for a plc and did part-time lecturing to trainee reps for the Tourism Training Organisation.

Starting in the lively resort of Benitses, she had to look after up to 250 people a week. At the airport she liaised with airline agents and coach companies and issued tickets. When there were delays she had to arrange refreshments and overnight accommodation, which often meant working a 24-hour day.

After meeting her clients, she organised a welcome meeting to tell them about the resort and sell excursions. This can be a very important part of a rep's duties, so it helps to be good at selling.

Once the clients were happily settled in to their accommodation, and Michelle had sorted out any complaints about rooms, she went to the resort office to confirm excursion bookings, write tickets and do paperwork. While in the office she helped callers who wanted to hire a car etc. Provided no one fell ill she might be lucky and finish by midnight!

Next day it would be office duties and then in the evening taking an evening excursion to a taverna where clients ate Greek food, saw a Greek floor show and drank Greek wine! Finishing by 2am, with any luck she would have the next day off until 7am the following day. This day was usually spent in hotel/villa visits, completing paperwork for the current group of clients, and checking that everything was all right for the next week's clients, finishing by 10pm.

One day there would be a beach barbecue, and Michelle helped to entertain the children, serve lunch, organise games and generally make sure the clients had a good time. After an exhausting day this was usually the time that something happened – from a car crash (hopefully minor) to stolen credit cards – and guess who had to help sort this out.

As well as with clients Michelle says you have to be very tactful when dealing with local hoteliers and villa owners. She had a lot of calming down to do the day one owner found out by chance that he wasn't going to be contracted for the next season – and refused to let any new arrivals in his property when the resort was fully booked.

In her next season Michelle started as a rep in Roda, but after two months was promoted to senior overseas rep for the Sidari/Roda area with 800 beds in total. She had to manage a team of five people, which included resort training and appraisals. As well as these duties she had to co-ordinate 20 reps at the airport for 15 incoming and outgoing flights each week.

Hilary had always wanted to be a rep and took the Westminster College course (now run by the Tourism Training Organisation). On the course she was given a list of over 400 companies that employed temporary staff as reps and guides and after 'over 50 phone calls' she came across Sunsail, a sailing tour operator, who offered her a job working as a receptionist/sub-manageress at a resort in Greece.

Her day started at 8am, liaising with new clients, telling them about the facilities and what was available. She had to order provisions for clients in self-catering accommodation and arrange for these to be delivered.

At lunch time she helped in the snack bar making sandwiches, and if she was lucky she had the afternoon off to go sailing, provided she was back by 5pm to open up the office and sell excursions, put out booking forms for sailing and tennis and then do the cashing up and banking.

Anyone wanting a babysitter would ask Hilary to organise this, and she also organised a baby listening service. She always had to be around to talk to clients who might want bed linen or towels, advice and information.

Change-over day saw her sorting out bills and making sure all villas and other accommodation were cleaned and ready for the next guests. Then it was on to the welcome meeting, explaining the weekly programme which included a Greek night, and Hilary's favourite: an evening trip to Cape Sunion to see the temple in the setting sun. Then there were themed and international nights, quiz night, posh night (glamorous frocks and gourmet cuisine) and of course the barbecue with spit roast, where she gave out certificates for sailing.

On top of this she organised birthday celebrations, car and mountain bike hire, and was always there to help solve problems from dripping taps or sunburn to more serious ones requiring a visit to the clinic or hospital. She must have enjoyed it though – asking her what she was going to do next summer there was an emphatic: 'Go back, I hope.'

The Giant Tour Operators

Without delving into the history of every major tour operator, let us just look at one giant and its background – Thomson Tour Operations, Britain's largest inclusive tour operator.

Thomson Tour Operations is part of Thomson Travel Ltd, the travel and holiday division of the International Thomson Organisation Ltd, which also controls newspapers and magazines, publishing, North Sea oil and other world-wide interests. The travel division itself operates its own airline, tour operating companies and a travel agency group.

When SkyTours, Riviera Holidays, Gaytours and Luxitours were amalgamated in the 1960s, they eventually formed Thomson SkyTours in 1970, which then became Thomson Tour Operations in 1972. That same year, the company acquired Sunair and Lunn Poly and the latter now operates over 350 retail travel outlets under the Lunn Poly name.

The continental department of Thomson Tour Operations looks after all aspects of overseas holidays. It is responsible for contracting aircraft and the accommodation used and provides those necessary services such as reps, baby patrollers, airport transfers and excursions. In high season, there are over 1,300 staff overseas, trained by this department. Quality control is also an important part of the continental department's work – monitoring all aspects of a holiday with the help of client-completed questionnaires.

Thomson passengers (in 1993 there were more than 3.3 million of them) can fly from 18 UK airports on the company's own airline, Britannia Airways, or on scheduled airlines from Heathrow to long-haul destinations.

It is the marketing department which has the role of producing the holiday brochures and ensuring customer awareness of Thomson products by advertising and public relations work. The sales division operates the reservations offices and promotes and sells through travel agents. The sales force distributes several million brochures to agents.

Thomson Tour Operations was the first company to introduce off-season weekend breaks in resorts normally only considered for summer holidays, and winter weekends to Majorca for £18 were announced in 1971. In 1972, Thomson's offered the first charter holidays from the UK to Jamaica and introduced weekends to Moscow from £29.

In 1973, cruising was launched and summertime holidays in established lake and mountain winter resorts were offered plus a programme of long weekend breaks in European capitals. Subsequently, Thomson's expanded into winter sports.

A fair trading charter was introduced the next year – a revolutionary move in terms of booking conditions, leading the way to proper public protection. A delay protection scheme, offering cash compensation and providing hotels and meals to holidaymakers delayed at the start of their holiday, was announced for summer 1979.

Advanced systems technology to streamline sales, reservations and booking administration is vital to every tour operator. It took three years and £3 million to develop the system Thomson's launched in 1976 when ten regional sales centres could communicate online with a powerful computer at head office via visual display units. In 1982, a reservations system called Thomson Open-Line Programme was made available to travel agents. Now over 6,000 agents are linked to the company by a TV screen using the latest Videotex technology. Direct computer links with the overseas resorts speed the administration even more and in 1987 Thomson's introduced an automatic banking system (TAB) to help agents save more administration costs.

The Self-Catering Tour Operator

Putting together the elements of a self-catering holiday is relatively new, but these days very popular. A self-catering package is where travel and accommodation arrangements are included, but not food. This covers a camping or caravanning programme, or a stay in a holiday apartment or a villa. It could comprise holiday cottages in the UK, or *gîtes*, as they are called in France, or something like a Greek taverna abroad (where accommodation is basic and food is available but not included in the holiday price).

Case Study

Jim Cuthbert and his wife Margaret are both founders of the company Canvas Holidays, and they are both graduates of Edinburgh University. Jim gained a law degree and Margaret an MA (Hons) in history. After a spell in America, Jim returned to Scotland to join a law practice, then to the Independent Broadcasting Authority as information officer and then to Rank Bush Murphy as a marketing executive. It was only after the couple were married and worked on the fledgling Canvas Holidays operation from the dining-room table, that it gradually grew into the £5 million business it is today.

By 1983, the company was offering 89 first-class camp sites, designed and developed to accommodate up to six people. Flexibility was the key, with holidaymakers coming and going on any day they pleased and staying for as long as they chose. Half of the permanent staff are graduates who look after the day-to-day running of the head office in Hertfordshire. Some 350 university graduates and undergraduates are employed in the summer as couriers.

Jim and Margaret developed their business enough to establish two subsidiaries: Car Holidays Abroad in 1970, for those who preferred hotel accommodation to canvas, and Cabin Holidays in 1983, which concentrated on self-catering holidays in Scotland.

The Cuthberts (who have since been joined by their sons, now directors) have always been innovators – with their tent equipment and facilities such as electric lights and toilets, to other new ideas such as their 1988 introduction of special interest camping holidays.

Here's what they say about the young people they look for to work for them:

As a courier you are expected to be a hard worker. Every tent or mobile home has to be thoroughly cleaned before the customer arrives, and you will need to be a practical person in case any of the equipment needs to be fixed. Practical, yes, but personable, too – you can, after all, make or break a customer's holiday. Tact and diplomacy are certainly essential attributes, but so is a happy disposition. Couriers are expected to visit the on-site guests and organise informal gatherings for both adults and children such as barbecues and wine and cheese parties, as well as run the twice-weekly Hoopi Club activities (treasure hunts, rambles, sports) for the youngsters.

A courier must also present a good appearance – that's why we provide the clothing for the job. Both your own tent and administration work (accounts, inventories etc) should also be in good order.

We receive thousands of applications annually for a courier's position, from whom we pick 300 either to work from the end of April to mid July, or mid July to the end of September. Our selection process starts in November and continues through June. During the November to March period, we hold regional interviews throughout Britain.

What type of person do we look for? Generally speaking, an undergraduate or someone taking a year off between school or university – so mostly the age range is 18-25 but we are flexible. Fluency in French, German, Italian or Spanish is certainly an incentive to us, but even without one of these languages, there may be another job for you. The 1993 wage is around £90 pw.

The same pay and conditions also apply to the children's courier, whose responsibility is to look after the young ones at certain times of the day and this may include babysitting. Previous teaching, nursery school or playgroup experience is very helpful here – language fluency is not.

We also need watersports couriers – previous experience in this area is necessary, and some professional qualification is preferred. Then we need what we call 'squaddies' who don't require language knowledge but must have physical strength and stamina, be able to work long hours under some pressure and live out of a rucksack, as they are the ones who put up and take down the tents on different sites. Additionally, full-time positions as area managers are available; based in our home office, at a salary of about £12,000 plus pa.

Qualifications

Currently all qualifications are being revised to become NVQs (National Vocational Qualifications). However, some sectors are used to working with specific qualifications, and these will continue to run side by side with NVQs for several years. That is why it is important to ask associations, employers and those working in the industry what qualifications are acceptable, and not just take the word of a college or awarding body.

The City and Guilds of London Institute have been chosen by ABTA to run their NVQs and can supply a list of suitable qualifications for tour operator staff and representatives. The Royal Society of Arts has a customer-specific Coach Tour Guides Diploma, which will eventually become an NVQ Travel Services (Guiding), and is also suitable for meet-and-greet staff.

If you like accounts and bookkeeping, many companies want qualified staff for resort offices. Under-21s can often obtain work as kiddies' reps if they have an NNEB *(Nursery Nurse Examination Board)* qualification or experience with children.

As the EC Directive on Package Travel requires reps to check safety in swimming pools, fire exits etc, it's no longer enough just to write to an operator hoping for a job – companies now look for staff 'who have invested in themselves' as Thomson says.

Other Qualifications

At Higher diploma or degree level, other qualifications, such as marketing and public relations, can be useful in tour operating although it is always worth looking at courses which concentrate on travel and tourism, as these other subjects may be offered as options on such a course.

Grants

Ask your careers officer or local education authority. There is a useful free booklet which they can obtain for you, 'Grants to Students: A Brief Guide'.

If you are unable to obtain a grant, there are career development loans. Phone 0800 585 505 for details. If you want to train abroad, read *Getting a Job in Europe* by Phillip Riley, (Northcote House Publishers; 0752 735251) which details help that might be available.

Unemployed?
There may be places available on Training for Work courses. Your local Jobcentre, Achievement through Training, the Training Academy and the Tourism Training Organisation will have details of what is currently available.

Chapter 2
Travel Agencies

What is a Travel Agent?

A travel agent is someone who sells tour operators' holidays, accommodation, transportation etc to the general public, thus acting as an intermediary between providers and buyers. In return, the travel agent receives a commission from the tour operator.

Travel agencies may be individually owned, be part of a chain, or in some cases owned by a tour operator. Through the knowledge and experience of their personnel they should be able to advise customers on best buys, suitable destinations and most convenient routes, as well as physically handling bookings and ticketing.

Although anyone can open a travel agency, that does not mean you can sell *any* product. Most reputable providers of holidays and holiday elements require that the agency they deal with has both an IATA licence and is an ABTA member.

What is ABTA?

The Association of British Travel agents was formed to help protect the general public. To become a member, the agent must pay 'bond' money, a safeguard in case he or she should fall into financial failure. All ABTA members agree to comply with codes of conduct which have been drawn up by ABTA in conjunction with the Office of Fair Trading. Since these codes have been created by travel industry specialists, they cover even remote contingencies, well beyond the requirements of the law.

ABTA regularly scrutinises the finances of its members; it demands that they employ properly experienced staff and contribute to a common fund. Tour operators are also usually members of ABTA and similarly abide by the EC Directive on

Package Travel, and by a code of conduct which covers matters such as procedures in the event of alterations, cancellations, surcharges or overbooking.

What is IATA?
The International Air Transport Association is the world organisation of the scheduled airlines of over 90 nations. Members co-operate with the International Civil Aviation Organisation; they often co-ordinate international tariffs and speak with one voice in their dealings with governments and other regulatory authorities.

Travel Agent Skills

A good travel agent not only books a package holiday for a client, or writes an airline ticket, but should also be able to organise all other forms of travel arrangement, including UK holidays, business and group travel. Some travel agencies will also expect their staff to sell travel insurance, foreign currency and travellers' cheques; organise a passport or visa for a customer's trip; arrange car hire of all sorts; possibly book theatre tickets.

Another skill necessary is the ability to deal with computers since an increasing number of travel companies are developing their own computer systems to enable agents to make instant bookings. In many ways, this makes work easier for agency employees, who can check availability and make immediate bookings direct with many tour operators, airlines, ferry companies, shipping companies, coach operators and car hire companies. The computer reservation systems enable agents to print out confirmation of a booking in minutes so that the customers may take it away with them instead of waiting to receive it through the post. Additionally, some of the computer systems can automatically suggest alternative holidays or call up extra information, such as insurance details, and show the full price before the booking is made.

Where Can You Go?

Vacancies for counter clerks and travel technicians (who put into effect the bookings made by the counter clerks) offer job opportunities for school leavers from the age of 16. At that age, you would be employed to handle the simpler aspects of the work, progressing to the more complex operational work as you gain experience. Larger travel agencies employ staff with qualifications and experience in accountancy, marketing and advertising and offer considerable prospects at their head offices for personnel with other professional and academic qualifications.

You might work towards becoming the manager of a single agency, several agencies or your own agency, or in time move to operations at head office with the eventual idea of becoming a company director (or managing director) or moving sideways into a tour operation.

Jobs and promotion will obviously go to those people with the right training, ability, appearance, personality and motivation. At any job interview, ask what training you will be given: for example, the employer would normally put you on the ABTA Youth Training programme at 16 or 17.

At some time during your training you would expect to start studying for ABTA-approved NVQ/SVQs.

Salaries are variable depending on location, on your expected responsibilities and on experience. Remember that a travel agency is a shop, albeit a shop selling a glamorous product. Starting pay is generally very low (see the advertisements on pages 13–16) and although you may be tempted with offers of free visits, these consist of familiarisation tours to an area where you *have* to visit 10 to 12 hotels every day and report back to your agency.

Bucket Shops

This is an awful name for what were once outfits selling cut-price airline tickets in dubious circumstances. Over the years some very reputable companies have come out of the bucket, and today dealing in 'consolidated' tickets can be handled by large, reputable companies. To work in this sector your geography must be spot on, and it helps to have a British Airways or IATA ticketing qualification.

Salaries are variable depending on location, on your expected responsibilities and on experience.

Case Studies
Kate had just joined a London travel agency as a trainee travel clerk at the time of this interview.

After I left school, I took a two-year full-time BTEC travel and tourism course at Thurrock College. Qualifications for this are four GCSEs at grades A-C, but if you wish to take the higher course, which is bilingual, you need at least two A levels, one of which must be a foreign language.

Thurrock has a very good reputation so a number of agencies will call when they have vacancies for juniors. At present I'm mostly involved with air ticketing, but I shall be working on inclusive tours and other elements for which I've been trained. I'm not sure what my ultimate aim is but a travel and tourism course does open a variety of doors in the travel industry, when it's followed by some practical experience.

Julie, at only 19, had the title of travel consultant at a travel agency which is not ABTA- or IATA-licensed.

I got my first job with a travel agency at 17. I only had one O level in English and some CSEs because my father is in the Forces and we'd moved about a great deal. How did I do it? I got out the *Yellow Pages* and listed every travel agency near where I lived – then I wrote to them all, asking if they had a position for a trainee. Most just sent application forms or said they'd let me know if something turned up, but one man was interested enough to call me for an interview. I think he was surprised I had shown initiative, and I was employed to do some typing and background bookings work.

Whatever you do you learn about the travel business and I was particularly interested in travel sales. When another employee opened her own company – The Trans-Continental Travel Company – she took me along with her. Because we are not ABTA-licensed you might call us a 'bucket shop', but bucket shops generally are so called because they buy tickets in bulk and sell them off cheaply. We, on the other hand, specialise in independent travel, particularly around the world. When someone calls me up with where they want to go, I let them know the best routeing and cheapest way of doing it, and organise their bookings. Our holding company, by the way, is ABTA/IATA so customers are reassured.

Qualifications

Basic qualifications that are useful for getting into training in travel agency work are several grades A-C at GCSE or SCE equivalents. These should preferably include subjects like English language, mathematics, geography and a foreign language. It is possible to get in with fewer qualifications, although the more you have the greater your advantage.

ABTA Youth Training

Each year ABTA arranges training and work experience for young people aged 16 to 18. There are currently more than 100 ABTA Youth Training programmes available, with 2,000 places for young people throughout the country each year. Training can take young people through to NVQ level 3.

To enter the programme, young people under 18 should contact travel agents direct, or can apply by filling in an application form which can be obtained from ABTA, who then contact participating employers with the names of interested young people. However, it is easier and quicker if first you try to find an employer willing to take you.

Entry into this kind of training is very competitive so it is always worth contacting employers direct, or considering, as an alternative to employment, a full-time course of study which is directly related to travel and tourism, and which has the ABTA seal of approval.

For details of training colleges and institutions offering travel courses, see Part 2.

Other Qualifications

Be very careful when choosing a course if it is *not* ABTA-approved. ABTA have been in the business of training for many years, and have won numerous awards for their training of young people.

There are reputable courses, although they do not have ABTA approval or recognition because they are designed for other sectors of the industry; then there are colleges that charge several thousand pounds for a course that has no validity in the UK. If in doubt, ask around employers and friends in the industry, contact ABTA or the appropriate association, and *listen* to their advice. We have all seen students crying because they have wasted money working for a 'diploma' that no reputable company will recognise.

College membership of a tourist board is *no* criterion; some Boards have to accept all membership applicants and have no way of checking courses.

British Airways Airline World Course

The objectives of this are to define IATA areas and IATA three-letter city codes; to plan an itinerary for any journey, giving accurate information about timings, connections, baggage allowances, aircraft types and airport facilities, flying times and red tape requirements; to calculate fares for single or multi-sector journeys both within the UK and abroad, and issue appropriate tickets; to handle bookings for special categories of passenger – for example pregnant mothers, invalids, unaccompanied minors etc.

Fares and Ticketing Course 1
The objectives of this course are to use the air tariff to quote all kinds of fares in local currency, for one-way, round trip, circle trip etc, using add-ons, certain routeings, mileage system and so on; to use IATA-ons, certain routeings, mileage system and so on; to use IATA-approved procedures to issue tickets for journeys of four flight sectors or less.

Fares and Ticketing Course 2
Open only to those who have already successfully passed Course 1, this is designed for those planning to sit the COTAC level 2 airline paper. Features include applying the fare construction principles learned in Course 1, plus calculating mixed class fares; determining the correct type of excursion or special fare for any routeing; correctly applying round and circle trip construction rules to world-wide excursion and other special fares; applying rebates for child, infant, youth and other special fares; applying flight, date, destination and/or stopover details by using revalidation slips or by re-issuing tickets; applying the correct currency procedures should the re-routeing result in an additional fare collection (in sterling or other currencies).

Other Courses on Offer

ABTA Package Holidays
This is a one-day course on package holidays and ancillary services, leading to a certificate awarded by ABTA National Training Board.

ABC Travel Guides
This is another one-day course on travel timetables recognised by the Institute of Travel and Tourism and ABTA, leading to a certificate from ABC International.

Travicom Computerised Reservations
A one-day training course is available for those who would be
using the Travicom Viewdata system in retail or business travel
agency work.

Costs

The air travel fares and ticketing courses last for anything
between two and ten weeks, depending on the level. They are
expensive, at £280 for one level or £810 for all three levels. Many
employers cover the cost of attending short courses to obtain
these qualifications, so it is very important not to commit yourself to a private course of study without first making sure you
have checked out all other ways of obtaining the necessary qualifications.

Chapter 3
Hotels

Hotels play a very big part in the travel industry. Tour operators must contract with them; travel agencies must book them. Tourists, business and conference groups all use them. Hotelkeeping and catering is itself one of the country's largest industries employing over 1.25 million men and women in UK establishments alone, thereby offering a multitude of job opportunities at all levels.

Hotelkeeping and catering is an international industry that includes job opportunities at airports, in leisure centres and holiday camps, and at convention centres and exhibition halls both at home and abroad. There is also a demand for catering on airlines, trains and cruise ships.

What Qualifications are Needed?

Depending on which aspect you choose, you may need anything from no qualifications to a degree in hotel management. GCSEs or their equivalents are always an advantage but they are not essential for entry into cookery, waiting, housekeeping, reception or a general catering course. They are, however, a must for management occupations, and the most helpful subjects are English language or literature, mathematics, science and any foreign business language.

Youth Training

The Hotel and Catering Training Company (HCTC), through their Caterbase scheme, together with the City and Guilds of London Institute (CGLI), organise training for young people to levels 1 and 2 at NVQ. Written and practical examinations are supplemented by assessment of achievements in the workplace.

Over 100 Caterbase modules are available to those who are in training. Full information about the training programmes is available from HCTC; you can write direct to HCTC or go to a careers office where information will also be available.

Picking the Right Area

Do you like people? Do you have no difficulty chatting and do you smile easily? Are you flexible and enthusiastic? Are you pleased with your personality and appearance? If the answers to these questions are 'yes', any of the careers where you meet the general public could be for you – that includes jobs at the reception desk and in the press office.

Are you academically terrible but good with your hands? Are you creative but shy? You do not have to be out in front for a position that involves cooking.

Do you love attention to detail, neatness and tidiness? A position in accounts, stores or stock-taking could be your answer. Or perhaps you may be best working for a hotel group or reservations system making bookings.

The possibilities are as endless as the prospects. If you are really not quite sure of which area to specialise in, first take a general course which provides school leavers with an introduction to the industry.

The Chef

There are all kinds of chefs working in all kinds of establishments, but there is no specific route to the top. You could get a job as an apprentice or trainee chef when you leave school, in which case you would probably attend a local college on day release for formal as well as practical training. Alternatively, you might opt for a two-year full-time training course to become a *commis* chef (assistant).

Case Study

Nick left school to become an apprentice in a large hotel kitchen. He is now *sous* chef (assistant to the head chef).

Initially, I was on day release at a local technical college for the formal part of my training. To be a chef, you must not only love cooking but be prepared for long hours, often on shift, to work hard and cope with hassles. In my present brigade [team of chefs] there are 12 people to cope with banqueting and restaurant meals. My job involves running the kitchen, from checking the supplies to planning with the head chef the menus for the next month. I supervise all the duties that need to be done in order to have food ready for service, though my special responsibility is training the *commis* chef and apprentices.

Nick still has to work a split shift and some weekends, though some hotels have two brigades. His eventual aim is to open his own restaurant.

The Waiter/Waitress

Food and beverage service will keep you very much in the public eye for longer periods than in any other type of catering work. Although no qualifications are compulsory, if you have an eye to job prospects in wine waiting or food and beverage management, training is essential.

Case Study
Kelvin is currently a master *sommelier* or wine waiter in a plush restaurant.

> I got a job as a waiter with no qualifications at all, but I was interested in wine so studied in my own time and took several exams set by the Guild of Sommeliers. To become a 'master *sommelier*' is to pass their top exam. I also hope to take a full-time hotel management course. At the moment, I work a split shift seven days a week. At the beginning of each duty spell, I check the stock of wines and see that the tables are properly laid with clean glasses and ashtrays. Service includes cocktails as well as wines and then liqueurs. A knowledge of food is helpful and enjoying people's company is essential. We are lucky here having two wine waiters and a *commis*, but in small restaurants you would be expected to wash glasses and clean up.

The Receptionist

A hotel receptionist may be one of a team of 20 or so working a rota system, checking customers in and out along with other duties that may include bookkeeping, handling cash and foreign exchange, taking reservations and dealing with accounts. Large hotels do sometimes employ staff aged under 18 in a junior capacity but since front office work is responsible, 18 is usually the minimum age.

Which Course?

Hotel staff, particularly those working for chains such as Sheraton, Hilton, Radisson, Forte, Mount Charlotte, Accor etc, are often moved around from place to place and country to country. Good training is essential, but personnel officers stress that it is the quality of the training rather than the qualification that they are looking for, ie a period in a hotel or kitchen under a general manager or head chef known to provide good training helps get the best jobs.

Time and again people mentioned the Hotel School at Lausanne, but mention was also made of training in Belgium, Germany, France and in the UK. A good hotel will ensure that you get time off to go to the local college to study for appropriate qualifications, such as City and Guilds in the UK. (See Chapter 1 for details of NVQs and SVQs.) Remember that training abroad can give you a language, which is essential in today's hotel industry.

Take the example of the Forte group, a British-based hotel and restaurant company that has become a world leader in the last 20 years. It runs development courses for graduates to prepare them for a management position, and programmes to train students for a responsible kitchen position in a hotel. Forte also runs what is usually a nine-month training period for the front office (reception). Depending on what level is being aimed for, Forte looks for the following qualifications:

A hotel and catering or tourism degree
A Hotel, Catering and Institutional Management Association (HCIMA) qualification
A postgraduate diploma in hotel-related studies
National Vocational Qualifications (NVQs levels 1 and 2 – previously City and Guilds certificates)
A BTEC Higher National Diploma – soon to be a GNVQ level 3.

You could find a secretarial or bookkeeping course helpful, and of course any business language training course.

Case Study

Jeannie took a full-time reception course on leaving school and is currently head receptionist in a large city hotel.

> How quickly you get promotion depends a little on luck and the size of the establishment. Turnover in this work is fast, however, so if you prove you are good you can become a head receptionist quite quickly,

as I did. In my job I am responsible for all the front office staff work – that includes the other receptionists, telephonists and reservations clerks. I organise the staff rota and help to select and train new staff.

You need a good personality and appearance, a good telephone manner – and patience. Its disadvantages are the long hours that can be disastrous for your social life, problems with guests – there are always some who cause problems but you can't be rude – and headaches if accounts don't balance. The advantage is that no two days are ever alike!

The Housekeeper

This is a job for a practical person who enjoys responsibility but does not seek to meet the public. You might start off as a junior or trainee in a large hotel straight from school, or you might work your way up from chambermaid (but this is a slow process). Promotion for an enthusiastic person can soon lead to a head housekeeping position when you will need to work closely with the reception and maintenance staff and supervise fully employed and casual room-cleaning labour.

Case Study

Rona joined a large northern hotel as a trainee housekeeper and took her CGLI 708 on block release. She is currently one of three assistant housekeepers.

Housekeeping duties vary according to establishment and numbers of full-time staff. Here, in addition to a head housekeeper and two other assistants, we have 13 room cleaners. I work on a rota system with my two colleagues which sometimes means starting the day as early as 6.30 am. If a chambermaid is away, it might mean cleaning rooms, too!

The most important element of the day is collecting the rooming sheet from reception which tells me which rooms have been occupied the night before and which guests are leaving that day. Linen checks are a must – for the current and following day. So are empty room checks – to make sure they have been cleaned properly, and that lights and other fixtures work. Reservations have to be checked for special requirements like flowers or champagne in the room or a cot. We also deal with guests' special requests like hair dryers or irons. A housekeeper needs to know a great deal about cleaning methods such as removing coffee or wine stains from carpets and curtains.

The Manager

Managers are needed in every department in a hotel from front office to food and beverage division. To become a general manager, you would usually need to have first worked in several of the departments at top level.

There are a number of different courses available to the potential management trainee from degree courses down. To become a manager you need a consuming interest and full commitment.

Which Course?

Degree Courses
There are many sandwich courses in hotel and catering management which involve a one-year placement in industry. Entry on to degree courses usually requires a minimum of two A-level passes, or four Scottish Higher grades. English, mathematics and a science may be expected at GCSE or Scottish Ordinary grade.

Postgraduate Courses
Postgraduate diplomas are available in some universities, polytechnics and colleges of higher education. These are usually one-year intensive courses for those who already hold a degree, but not necessarily in a related subject.

Case Studies

Geoff worked in hotels of all kinds and at all levels before reaching his present position as manager of a large city centre hotel.

> I joined a hotel chain straight from school and spent six years training, going through all the departments. I spent three subsequent years abroad in different countries before returning to the UK. Then I spent two more years in British hotels before joining this one five years ago. It usually takes a long time to reach top management level and these days much of my work is administrative.
>
> Under me there's a deputy manager, an assistant manager, a personnel officer, food and beverage manager and banqueting manager. They are all heads of department but I oversee their work. When you're a hotel manager there are no set hours – it depends on what work is at hand. The day usually starts with the post and the duty manager's report on the previous night's occupancy and any problems that might have arisen. There's usually a daily meeting for

heads of department but, apart from that, each day is completely different. Though I delegate work, in the end it's my responsibility.

Martin chose quite a different area of management, and is currently assistant manager at a motorway service area.

When I left school, I did a two-year full-time junior management course in hotel and catering studies. Then I went into hotel management for two years prior to coming here. The hours now are regular ones although I do have to work many weekends and sometimes visit night shifts. The rest of the staff work a split shift as we're open 24 hours a day, seven days a week. Because we're in the commercial fast food business – people don't come here for an expensive meal – there's a different set of organisational problems from those in a hotel, but the job's a challenge I enjoy.

Sales and Marketing

The careers we've talked about so far in the hotel industry are all 'operational', but another large area is sales and marketing. Every hotel has a sales team and hotel chains additionally have group sales and marketing departments, both on a national and, when appropriate, international level. A large hotel is likely to employ its own public relations or press officer and here, again, international chains will also have a group public relations office.

Qualifications for this side of the industry are the same initially as for any other industry: an outgoing, positive attitude; precise and forward thinking; a smart appearance and likeable manner. There are numerous sales and marketing courses available. One of your best bets is to read *Careers in Marketing, Advertising and Public Relations* in this series.

Hotel Group Marketing

How does this relate to the travel industry? Many hotel groups or consortiums produce their own holiday packages, especially in the UK. These are then sold through travel agents to the public just like any inclusive programme. In a case like this, the hotel's marketing team works closely with transportation (car hire companies or perhaps British Rail) and with the print and production team to produce annual brochures.

The Hotel Consortium

'Consortium' is the name given to a group of unrelated hotels (ie, usually independently owned) who generally cannot afford their own sales/reservations office. By becoming what in effect is a group, they can save time and money and make more of an impact on the market. Bookings for any of the members are taken in one place. Marketing and public relations efforts for all and any members stem from one office.

More often than not, member hotels will have something in common. Perhaps they are all country house hotels or historic house hotels. Perhaps they have a certain luxury standard or maybe they are all town house hotels.

Hotel Group Reservations

Large international hotels have their own reservations service; others will use a world-wide reservations service such as Utell. In almost all cases, training is done in-house. What qualifications should you have when you apply for a reservations job? Certainly, a good educational background is necessary (Hilton Reservations Service looks for young people with a minimum of four GCSEs). A general knowledge of geography is important since you will be dealing with reservations for places around the globe, and any previous hotel background is helpful in understanding the product and possible booking problems.

You will be on the telephone a lot so a pleasant conversational manner is necessary and, since you may well be talking to executives, a mature and efficient-sounding approach is equally essential. These days, 99 per cent of reservations offices use computers so a basic computer course is beneficial. But, remember that each hotel group has its own procedures so that, as Hilton Reservations Service points out, a person trained in Sheraton reservations will have to be retrained for Hilton.

Hotel Representation

Hotels which do not have their own reservations or sales office may choose a hotel representative to act on their behalf. Hotel representation, as opposed to a straightforward booking service, invariably involves public relations, sales and marketing as well as reservation taking, so that job prospects are better and career choice more exciting. The hotel representative will only take on hotels of a similar nature or alternatively concentrate on a particular part of the world. Work involves liaison with tour operators, travel agencies, the press and the individual hotels themselves.

Other Means

In addition to the recognised colleges and courses, private education centres also offer relevant training. But don't forget, many hotel chains train within – at all levels, even from the bottom up. Forte Hotels, for example, is a British-based hotel company moving from strength to strength. It runs development courses for graduates, to prepare them for a management position. It runs a three-year programme to train students for a responsible kitchen position in a Forte hotel. It runs what is usually a nine-month training period for the front office.

Chapter 4
Airlines

So you want to work with the airlines, but where do you start? There are many areas from operational to administrative. Engineering, catering or sales could all lead to an airline career. You could become a pilot or a steward/stewardess, or work at an airport. Or you could take telephone reservations or meet and greet VIPs. Many of these jobs involve shift work, for which the minimum age is 18.

Administration

British and foreign airlines run administrative offices in the UK. They all employ telephonists, receptionists and secretaries. They all have a sales manager and/or sales team, plus a marketing manager and/or marketing division. In some cases they will have their own public relations office; in others they will use the services of an outside public relations agency. They all liaise with an advertising agency and operate a ticketing office.

Airline headquarters in the UK have personnel, financial and promotional divisions and, in British Airways, their own tour operation sectors. All major carriers have their own ticket desks at Heathrow and/or Gatwick.

Operations

In addition to those who fly and work on the planes, there is airport work. The airports have their own administrative teams too, of course, but ground handling might mean anything from meeting a celebrity off a flight to handling groups or unaccompanied children, or coping with an emergency.

Catering also comes under the operational banner – in the

airport itself and for the airlines. And cargo handling is yet another possibility.

The Steward/Stewardess

This is probably the easiest job to obtain in the airline world, but even so there are hundreds of applications for just one vacancy. Luckily for job hunters the turnover is high, so write to as many airlines as possible, applying to be trained. (Airlines train their own stewards and stewardesses.)

Entry requirements for cabin crew vary slightly between airlines but usually they require a minimum height of between 5ft 2in and 5ft 4in, a pleasing appearance with weight in proportion to height, and an education that includes some GCSEs/SCEs. Successful applicants must also pass a medical. Good English and reasonable ability in at least one other language is certainly a help and any previous experience in nursing, teaching or catering is beneficial. Stewards/stewardesses are usually aged 19 to 30. Airlines will accept those wearing contact lenses. Many also require that you are able to swim a certain distance wearing clothes.

The thought of seeing and staying in destinations you could never afford gives a cabin crew career its glamour, but in fact it is not quite the glamorous job you might think. People who tell you that it is 'glorified waiting' are only too right. There is the benefit of travel, but not every route takes you to an exotic destination and not every stopover is long enough for you to enjoy it. Flying so frequently can upset the bodily system (particularly for women) and even when you are not flying, you may be 'on call', ie available for work at a moment's notice. Working unpredictable hours can also play havoc with any social life.

The airlines run their own full-time training courses for newly accepted staff, which may last up to six weeks. During that time such subjects as galley management, customer relations, first aid and emergency procedures are covered, as well as the serving of food and beverages. Advanced training usually follows after several months' flight experience, and refresher courses are given from time to time.

Case Study

Tracy works as a stewardess on domestic and short-haul flights to Europe.

Training is quite involved. You learn emergency procedures, cabin service and first aid. I was even shown how to survive in the desert and the Arctic. At the end of the course there's an exam which requires a 96 per cent pass mark. If the airline flies several different types of aircraft, each with its own procedures, you must learn all of them. You must also know the duties of each member of the cabin crew so that, in an emergency, you could take over from them. Every year there's a refresher course, a line check on each aircraft and a spot check.

On short flights, you rarely get to stay anywhere since you're out on one flight and back on the next, but working in the airline business does give us opportunities to buy cheaper holidays. It's really harder work on short flights when you maybe only have an hour to serve over 70 passengers with drinks and food. Galley space is minimal so you need to keep everything neat and tidy. Chief stewards/stewardesses also have to do quite a bit of paperwork – an element of the job that trainees sometimes forget.

Reservations and Ticketing

Airlines, like other travel organisations, tend to train their own staff for reservations and ticketing procedures. These days, one of the most important factors is the ability to work with computers.

Case Study
Jennie worked, until recently, for South African Airlines in reservations, though the airline sent her on a ticketing course.

I started my career with no formal training, leaving school at 16 with some O levels to work at Thomas Cook. They asked me what I wanted to do and I told them 'a booking clerk'. But all the other school leavers wanted to do the same, and being the most junior I had to start at the bottom as a mail clerk. In a large organisation like Cook's, there are many areas for promotion. I moved to being a debitor, then an itinerary clerk, then an individual inclusive itinerary clerk – checking a traveller's itinerary, making bookings for hotels, car hire etc. I left Cook's to join the reservations team at Middle East Airlines who trained on the spot. At that time it was a manual system. Then I went on to South African Airways where I was retrained in computer systems.

Ground Staff

When airlines recruit ground staff they look for people aged between 20 and 30, and who are used to dealing with the general public. They must have a general standard of GCSE/SCE education and since (like cabin staff) it is a uniformed job, weight must be in proportion to height. Another language is helpful. Successful applicants then go on a four-week in-house training course. Since an airline like BA promotes from within, many ground staff (including the special unit which handles VIPs etc) are recruited from former air hostesses.

Case Study

Tessa was a stewardess with Britannia Airways until recently, and has now moved to the administration unit as ground staff.

> My stewardess job was my first since school; I got the job by applying to an ad in the paper. They required English O level and two other O levels. After sending in an application with photo, I was called with several others for an interview. They talked to us individually about our family and social life and then gave us a simple maths test. After that they split us into small groups to work on an imaginary plan of campaign involving travel arrangements. If you pass all that and your weight and measurements are all right, you also have to take a medical before you are taken on as a trainee.

In Tessa's case the course was a three-week one that included first aid (with an exam) and training for emergencies and cabin sales before she 'got her wings'.

> You start as a three or four – ie, there's a number one head stewardess who takes care of most of the paperwork; a number two who does the Customs paperwork and then a three or four. For the first three flights, a really senior stewardess checks you out and, for the first three months, you're subject to constant assessments. We worked on a roster so we knew three weeks in advance which routes we were on – either in the UK or abroad, averaging a stopover only once in six weeks.

Tessa's current job is as co-ordinator checking the assessments of new girls.

Working at Airports

Not all the airports are the same so jobs can vary as can titles. In some cases, it is the airport operator who is the employer (for management, administration, baggage handling, maintenance, cleaning, information, apron control, medical and emergency services). Other employers may be private companies based at an airport (careers here might include catering, car hire etc).

Airline traffic staff need at least four GCSE/SCEs or equivalent and must be over 18. Some airlines offer a general training scheme which encompasses accounts, cargo, reservations, passenger services, computer operations and personnel. In most cases, airlines offer four-year maintenance engineering apprenticeships.

Competition for an air traffic control position is fierce. The Civil Aviation Authority (CAA) has a Cadet Entry Scheme for which candidates must be aged 18 to 26 and have at least two A levels or three SCE Higher grades including maths or a science. Cadets are selected by tests and interviews. Entry into Customs and Excise or immigration careers is by the Civil Service entry exam.

The British Airports Authority recruits graduates for training in computing, finance and management services and the CAA sometimes recruits people with previous experience in airport operation, for managerial positions. If your aim is to become an airport manager, you might consider diplomas in business studies which include transport options. Degree courses in transport administration, management and planning are offered by a number of universities and polytechnics. Contact the Chartered Institute of Transport for further information.

Chapter 5
Tourism and Tourist Offices

What is a Tourist Office?

A tourist office is a country's representative abroad whose main function is to provide the general public with information regarding that country. Other functions involve working with airlines, travel agents, hotels, stores and the media for promotional activities. Most major countries support a tourist office in the UK.

The director (and deputy if any) is almost always a native of the country represented, as are the majority of the staff – though the latter may live permanently in the UK. In some cases, the director might stay for years in the same post but, more frequently, is in a term of office for three or four years before being relocated.

Career Opportunities

A number of tourist offices employ a public relations officer who may or may not originally be from the country being represented. If not, a knowledge of the language is almost always demanded. Sometimes an outside public relations agency will be used, in which case language may not be a requisite. Also, a tourist office generally uses an advertising agency and sometimes will have its own publications department. In a few cases, there may even be a conference or business group specialist.

The main job opportunities for British school leavers, however, are as secretaries or counter staff (information officers) and, of course, telephonists. Secretarial skills apart, there is no defined way of entry to work in a foreign tourist office, though obviously a knowledge of the country concerned is going to give you an edge.

The British Tourist Authority

The prime job of the British Tourist Authority (BTA) is to promote Britain to overseas visitors. They do this through representatives in different countries. Therefore, the main function is marketing within which there are other divisions: business, incentive and conference travel; a press and public relations office; film and TV and radio division; production services; publications; distribution.

With the exception of clerical staff, most of the people working here are specialists in their field, though their backgrounds are extremely diverse. Journalistic or marketing experience is frequently desirable.

National Tourist Boards

The National Tourist Boards' function is to promote their own country to visitors so, like the BTA, the main role of the English, Irish, Scottish and Welsh Tourist Boards is marketing. Under this heading come departments like planning and research, and sales and distribution, as well as sectors which deal with publications, the press and the travel trade.

A division called special facilities handles promotions and events while the external relations division liaises with the regional tourist boards and their own press and public relations. Special projects and finance come under a research and development banner, and central services involve personnel, office services, computerised operations and information officers.

The English Tourist Board

The English Tourist Board (ETB) is particularly enthusiastic about promoting jobs in the tourist industry, and publishes, as part of its information service, several helpful careers information sheets for school leavers from age 16 to university graduate age.

Regional Tourist Boards

England is split into 11 regions, each of which boasts its own tourist board – a division of the ETB. Work involves marketing that specific region with the aid of promotions, publicity, events and sometimes conference services. Staffing is not large and competition for vacancies, when they arise, is stiff.

Tourist Information Centres (TICs)

Tourist information centres are scattered throughout the UK in places of visitor importance. They may range from a small, centrally located kiosk to an office with several employees. These are the places to which the general public comes seeking information – where to stay or eat, how to get to a certain attraction or site, what events are taking place that day and so on. The information office may produce its own written material for tourist guidance, but is more likely to act as a distributor. Staff are generally locals with a good knowledge of the immediate area. Having a bright and friendly personality is an asset. Most of the work is of the counter variety though some officers occasionally may be expected to show visiting agents, press or VIPs around. Work is often seasonal.

With over 800 TICs scattered around Britain, there may be work for you locally, particularly if you speak a foreign language. Competition for jobs is fierce, and in somewhere like London or Edinburgh you won't even get an interview unless you speak two or more European languages, or a 'scarce' one such as Japanese.

Case Study

Alan says no two days are the same, but the most usual question visitors ask is 'Where are the toilets?' Although the work involves dealing with the public, there are a lot of boring things to do such as replenishing the racks with literature which he is sure walks out the door on its own.

The leaflets are free, but there are books to sell, theatre tickets and BABA – Book a Bed Ahead – for people travelling round without room reservations. Most people ask him 'Which is the best hotel available?' but he is not allowed to give recommendations, and has to operate a strictly fair system of booking allocations.

Funnily enough, many callers are locals wanting information

about what is happening in the area. Even though Alan thought he knew the area well, there is always something new to discover. Callers not only need to know what is available locally, but ask about the regions around, and even further afield, so the English Tourist Board runs two to three day familiarisation trips for TIC staff. These are great fun; everyone stays in a good hotel and is taken around by coach for a guided tour of the area selected and Alan gets to chat to his colleagues who are usually only a voice on the phone. He discovers they all have hilarious stories of visitors wanting to know 'Am I in Italy?' and 'Why did the Queen build Windsor Castle under the Heathrow flight path?'

Winter should be a quiet time, but with tour operators and hotels selling inexpensive weekend breaks, TICs in the tourist honeypot towns are often almost as busy as in summer.

Stock-taking or letter-writing – Alan has to do it all so there is a lot of administrative work but all in all it's very interesting, with each visitor wanting something different.

How can you Work for a Tourist Office?

There is simply no precise way or guaranteed training that will get you a position with a tourist board or information centre. It really is as much a question of luck as of judgement. An English or other language degree, a marketing degree or writing ability can be extremely useful if you have aspirations to reach the top, but do not dismiss the backdoor route of office work, accountancy or personnel.

City and Guilds have designed courses in tourism which lead to a COTICC certificate of competence for tourist information staff, but you need a job first before you can take this part-time programme.

Other Opportunities

Every tourist attraction needs people to promote it, write about it, market it and show people around. The range is a very wide one, from historic houses and museums to marinas, recreational areas and safari parks. A museum curator or assistant almost undoubtedly needs specialised experience, for example a study of history, sociology, archaeology etc. But, for those out to market it, a sales background is preferable.

The Tourist Guide

Unfortunately, it is not as easy to be a tourist guide as you might anticipate. It is not just a question of knowing your home town well, but one of age and competing with a host of hopefuls to get accepted on a training course that leads to a 'blue or green badge' guide qualification.

Regional tourist boards (including the London Tourist Board) run courses of varying lengths for tourist guides but there are always hundreds of applicants. The London Tourist Board, for example, runs an annual part-time course for 35 candidates over a two-year period. You must first fill in an application form, then attend a pre-interview test on general knowledge relevant to guiding. If you are successful at that, you will then be called for an interview proper when you will be assessed mostly on personality, appearance and attitude. At the end of the course, there is a stiff written and practical exam which, when passed, gives the 'blue or green badge' nationally recognised qualification.

Although there are no specific educational requirements, tourist boards usually look for candidates in the 25 to 55 age bracket. Some areas, where the need for tourism is great, may accept younger people, especially if they speak a business language, or may run only a one- or two-week course. A working committee for regional tourist boards has drawn up a national standard of requirements for guiding which it hopes will eventually be accepted by all tourist boards, leading to NVQ/SVQs. Registered (blue or green badge) guides can be town, city or regional guides who are generally self-employed, working on a daily basis from home.

Other guides may work as site guides for agencies such as English Heritage, trail guides working in national parks, house guides who are employed by stately homes and the National Trust, walking tour guides based in an historic or specially interesting town or area, guides for churches, abbeys and cathedrals, museum guides etc. Generally, these guides are trained by their employers, who are helping to develop NVQ/SVQs, or they have taken a course for the RSA Diploma.

Now that people are so interested in finding out how other people work, there can be job opportunities in local factories taking round groups of the public, shareholders and overseas VIPs. Whoever would have thought that a visit to a nuclear power station would be so popular, but Sellafield has a team of guides.

Once guides were mostly unpaid volunteers, but today's visitor expects a high standard of guiding which has led to employers hiring more professional staff.

Coach tour guides take groups from place to place on tours of the UK or Europe, lasting a weekend or up to several weeks. You have to be free to stay away from home while on tour, and may work just for the summer, although today many coach tour operators have work throughout the year especially those offering weekend breaks. Again the RSA Diploma is useful, while waiting for the level 2 NVQ to be up and running.

Returners, Retired and Changing Career

There are an infinite variety of special interest tours: for the over-60s, newspaper reader offers, art lovers' and historical tours, tours to battlefields, to trade exhibitions, and over eight million coach travellers cross the Channel each year on a tour.

Work is usually part time until you become known, but then it is up to you to decide how many days you want to work.

People considering a second, or even third, career, will often find experience from their previous job can be put to very good use. So if you were a policeman, in the Armed Forces, like flower arranging, sewing, or have any one of a thousand hobbies, there is probably a company that would be interested in offering you part-time work as a guide. Just take a basic course and start phoning!

The Tour Manager

After one or two seasons a coach tour guide will be deemed experienced enough to look after more demanding groups such as special interest tours for art and history lovers, or to take foreign visitors around the UK or on the Continent, and become a coach tour manager or director. Eventually, there will be NVQs at levels 3 and 4 as a qualification.

Case Study

Bob took a course for the RSA Diploma, and 'I'm glad I did, because on my first tour the ferry was late and it had been dinned into us that we *must* phone to let hotels etc know of delays'. The hotel manager was very pleased because the week before the same thing had happened and no one had let him or his staff know.

Bob takes British people abroad for weekend breaks and ten-day holidays to Austria and Italy. 'It's a bit of a rush, and next year I hope to be good enough to work for a company that offers more leisurely art tours.' But Bob enjoys the variety, being his own boss and making sure that his 40 passengers have a wonderful holiday.

His day starts with a wake-up call at 6.30. It's breakfast in his bedroom because once outside 'the problems start' and he needs a cup of coffee before he can get going. Then it's down to the dining room to ensure everyone is having breakfast, and a good morning handshake with his Belgian driver. While this is going on the porters are bringing down the luggage, ready for the driver to load on to the coach once Bob has triple-checked the number tallies.

Having collected everyone and made sure they have paid their extras bills and left hotel keys behind, it's off on the day's tour by coach which usually includes one visit to a castle or house, venue or museum, and travelling through interesting countryside. Bob reckons he is giving a commentary about 25 per cent of the time, talking about everything that might interest his group regarding history, local life and customs, economic development, local flora and fauna and anecdotes.

Lunch time is a bit harrowing; Bob has to find somewhere for everyone to eat where they can get sandwiches, the loos are clean, and there aren't too many shops for his group to get lost in! His favourite stop is at one of the many large tourist shops, with a good coffee shop, telephones and loos all under one roof – and coach parking to keep his driver happy.

During the day they may stop at an interesting wayside church, have a guided tour of a famous town with a local guide, and then arrive at their hotel about 6pm.

After dinner Bob may take the group on a walking tour, or if there are lots of bars and discos, leave them to their own devices while he escapes to his room to check all the details for the next day such as phoning the hotel, the guide and anywhere else they may be visiting. Then he gets out his guidebooks to update his commentary for the next day and check facts and details. With luck, and no problems from anyone who has fallen sick in the night, he gets to sleep about midnight before the next 6.30 alarm call.

Chapter 6
Cruise Lines

Working on a ship could prove to be a fascinating experience. It could take you to far corners of the globe or act as interim work experience before you finally settle on a career. Although cruise ships try to employ nationals wherever possible, foreign passenger lines do require some British staff if they are selling to the British travelling public.

Career Opportunities

Administrative work for a shipping line includes office duties, sales and marketing, press and public relations, and reservations. On the operational side, the main jobs are for caterers, stewards and pursers. Entertainers are in constant demand and, of course, ships do have their own medical and engineering teams. Large cruise liners require hairdressers, sales people for their shops and boutiques, and croupiers when they have a casino on board.

The advantages of working at sea are obvious, but do remember the disadvantages: stewards and pursers may have to work seven days a week with little free time; hairdressers and sales staff (unlike officers, entertainers and social hostesses) do not mix with the passengers; space is restricted and the wrong type of person stuck on board for weeks at a time (as one young hairdresser told us) could go 'stir crazy'.

The Steward/Stewardess

Stewards might work on a passenger or cargo ship. On the former, their tasks tend to be specialised, such as serving in the restaurant or working in the pantry or stores. On the latter, they could well be expected to clean, make beds etc, besides serving meals.

Basic catering training (for young men and women) is given at the National Sea Training College, Gravesend, but any catering training is worth while before going to sea.

All catering personnel must be registered with the Merchant Navy Establishment Administration and be members of the National Union of Seamen. A shipping company is able to recommend waiters and bar stewards for membership if they have at least 18 months' experience in a hotel or restaurant and/or have successfully completed the City and Guilds of London Institute exam in general catering, 7050, or relevant NVQ/SVQ.

Promotion is generally from within, so a waiter could move on to become section waiter, assistant head waiter and then head waiter. Alternatively, promotion might lead to public room steward, assistant barman, public room barman and then bar services manager. Or you might be considered as a bedroom steward, which leads to assistant accommodation supervisor, then accommodation supervisor.

A cruise line will provide food and accommodation free and will usually grant up to ten days' leave per month served on board, but you will be expected to pay for your own uniform. The minimum age is 20.

Kitchen Staff

A cruise line chef is responsible for a great deal of food preparation for a large number of people. With an eye to this career, you would be starting as a number three cook, butcher or baker with a company like P & O. Qualifications for third cook are City and Guilds Cookery for the Catering Industry passes 706/1 and 706/2 or relevant NVQ/SVQ, and some practical experience in a top-class establishment. The minimum age is 20.

Your duties might involve the preparation and cooking of fish or grills, or you may be the stove cook. You may be requested to assist the larder cooks or be given the position of crew pantryman.

As a third baker, you will need City and Guilds in bakery, 1301, catering college training in all aspects of baking, or completion of an apprenticeship as a baker. Duties might involve assistance with the preparation of sweets, with the making of breads, or in the dairy section.

As a third butcher, you must first have served apprenticeship in a meat and poultry establishment. Work will involve dissecting and preparing joints and cuts of all types of meat, plus freezer work.

In all cases, food and accommodation are free but you have to provide standard working clothes.

The Purser

The purser is head of what, these days, cruise ships call 'hotel services afloat', and is responsible directly to the captain. It is a job that requires excellent organisational abilities plus diplomacy; helping passengers calls for patience, courtesy and tact. The purser's bureau answers questions and enquiries, cashes travellers' cheques and deals with all the documentation and the crew work of the ship, so accounting and clerical skills are essential.

Initial recruitment is as junior assistant purser either for administration or for catering. Qualifications for the former are secretarial skills – 55 wpm typing and 120 wpm shorthand – and reception and cash handling experience. Knowledge of a continental language is an advantage. Entry to the catering side demands graduate membership of the Hotel, Catering and Institutional Management Association, or the Higher National diploma in hotelkeeping and catering operations, plus a minimum of one year's full-time practical experience.

Applicants must be aged between 21 and 26 and will be requested to attend a preliminary interview and a selection board, and pass a medical before acceptance.

Promotion leads to the title of assistant purser whose duties are similar but with added responsibilities. From there the ladder is to senior assistant purser and then to deputy purser. The deputies take care of victualling, service to passengers and control of the crew. The deputy purser (catering) oversees the chef's side of things (kitchen organisation, preparation and cooking of food, ship's storerooms), while the deputy purser (accommodation) looks after the passenger's cabin service, dining and other public rooms.

Junior assistant pursers earn paid leave at around 229 days per service year. During their first six months at sea they will be assessed, after which there is an interview and review of career prospects. Officers in the purser's department are expected to pay for their own uniforms.

Deck Cadets

The normal requirement is four GCSE (grade C or above) or SCE Standard grades at 3 or above. These should include a science-related subject, mathematics, and a subject demonstrating use of English. (Slightly lower entry qualifications are asked for by the Small Ships Training Group.) Applicants with higher qualifications such as A levels or Scottish Higher grades can get into an accelerated training scheme. Training for those starting under 18 is split into periods spent at sea and time spent at college, and lasts for three to four years. Deck cadets are also required to have normal vision in form and colour.

Engineering Officers

Entry requirements are similar to those required for deck cadets, with physics being a preferred subject. Training lasts for four years, with the first year being spent in college, the second at sea, and the rest split between the two. It is also necessary for engineering cadets to have reasonable eyesight and good colour vision.

It is possible to do a course of training which leads to both deck and engineering officer qualifications. For this, it is necessary to have A levels or Scottish Highers with mathematics, physics and one other subject passed, and the training takes an extra 18 months.

Radio/Electro-Technical Officers

Entrants are required to have four GCSE/SCE Standard grades, including mathematics and English and preferably physics. Courses can be taken at colleges belonging to the Association of Marine Electronic and Radio Colleges, which lead to BTEC Higher qualifications in Electronic and Communications Engineering. After two years (the course lasts for three) the BTEC National diploma in Telecommunications may be obtained. SCOTVEC offer a Higher qualification in Electrical and Electronic Engineering (Radio and Radar) with Marine Options.

Other Possibilities

A registered general nurse with a registered midwife certificate could find work on board a cruise ship. A qualified infant or junior school teacher might find a position as a children's hostess. Printers, telephonists and cinema projectionists are also called for.

Recruitment

Send an sae to one of the major cruise lines. There is tremendous competition for jobs and, once accepted, there can be a wait of up to two years before a berth (place) becomes available.

However, the Florida coast and the Caribbean are becoming very popular for cruising, and ships plying out of Miami often need staff. They recruit via agencies in Britain, which often advertise in *Overseas Jobs Express.*

A typical advertisement reads:

> **USA/WORLDWIDE CRUISES**
> Waiters, sommeliers, bartenders, bar waiters/ess and chefs (all grades) required for USA/world-wide cruises. High tax-free salaries. Applicants must be aged over 21 and have 2 to 3 years' experience in first-class establishments.
>
> Send CV, employment references and 2 photographs now, to:

Be prepared for a very searching interview and, if accepted, you will have to pay for a return air ticket to Miami valid for one year (much more expensive than an excursion ticket). Cruise operators have had their fingers burnt with staff arriving from Europe and either jumping ship or else deciding that the work was too hard and having to be sent home. So now they insist that you have the means to return so they are not out of pocket.

Chapter 7

Other Holiday Operations

The travel and holiday industry includes tourist attractions, theme parks, wildlife parks, national parks, conservation, gardens, and many other interesting job opportunities. When it comes to courses you can take to help you on your way, remember that although tourism may be one of the oldest industries in the world (St Paul probably wrote the first travelogue) it's very new when it comes to training.

The Institute of Baths and Recreational Management runs courses for the leisure and recreational industry. Then there are in-house and day-release courses for operational staff at visitor attractions etc. The Institute of Leisure and Amenity Management has introduced a certificate and diploma qualification, and there are also degree courses in leisure and recreation at an increasing number of higher education centres.

Boating Holidays

A boating holiday does not necessarily mean cruise ship work. If you have ever taken a boating holiday in England, you will realise there is a wider range. Britain has over 2,000 miles of waterways: the Midlands, for example, has more miles of canals than Venice, while the favourite stretches continue to be the Norfolk Broads, the Thames, the Avon and the Scottish waterways.

Blakes is one of the leading operators in this holiday field, having started in 1908. This is a managing company which acts as agent for around 100 independent boat hire companies. Some are small, family-owned businesses; others are much larger with a limitless choice of boats. As managing agent, Blakes sets the standards (with which every boat must comply), produces a brochure and takes the bookings. The company, therefore, has its own managing director and marketing team, representatives and reservations staff. A public relations agency conveys the company's message. Like all operators or agents worth their salt, Blakes continually looks to expand its programme. For example, in 1984 it introduced international boating holidays that included the rivers and loughs of Ireland, French and Dutch waterways, and flotilla sailing in Greece and the Adriatic.

Blakes has to cost and negotiate with boatyards and owners, so people with an accountancy background are needed. Since it is a direct-book firm, it operates a telephone booking service seven days a week.

Hoseasons (another well-known agent for boating companies) distributes its brochures via Martins the Newsagent and travel agencies, as well as keeping its traditional direct-sell aspect. A company marketing exercise in 1984 meant that additional brochures were promoted in 200 selected post offices and that the public could choose their holiday from Littlewoods stores all over the UK.

Innovative ideas are a must in the travel industry. Hoseasons, for instance, expanded into holiday homes, first on a self-catering level and then with meal-inclusive programmes at eight holiday centres providing daytime activities and evening entertainment. The company introduced the term 'country club centres', which are self-catering homes based around a manor or castle where country club style facilities are available.

There are also jobs relating more directly to boating: one could be called on to skipper or crew a boat, for example. Sailing enthusiasts might put their hobby to profitable use, and become flotilla leaders or part of the team. Basic catering knowledge is useful for boating holidays where everything is done for the passenger. Further expansion of thought brings in the watersport centres – sailing instruction, maintenance, starting up a windsurfing school etc.

Holiday Centres

Organisations such as Butlins, Pontins etc no longer call themselves holiday camps, but holiday or leisure centres. What they provide is a totally inclusive programme with a schedule of activities, events and entertainment. On the in-house side, they must market, sell and promote. On-site, they must manage, cater for, and look after the holidaymakers. A nursing or child-care background could be beneficial; experience as a sports instructor is also useful. Other areas of work include kitchen and bar staff, and food and beverage control. The ability to organise and an outgoing personality are assets for the job of 'Redcoat' or entertainer.

A teaching background does not limit you to work in schools. These days, speciality interest/training is needed for hotel and holiday centre vacations. Activity courses are very popular on the holiday scene, whether it be photography, flower arranging, riding, painting or computer knowledge.

Health Clubs

Health is such a topical subject that it has turned into a profitable industry of its own. But health clubs do not always have to be severely medical – they are also geared to relaxation and leisure. A beauty or nutritional training could lead to a job with an independent health club – they are scattered all over the country, but are especially predominant in London. It could also lead to a job in a hotel health club but you will need first aid training. Practically every new hotel being built has its own health centre with pool, jacuzzi, sauna, steam rooms, gym and massage rooms. Even the older established hotels have added these facilities, and require personnel with expertise to run and work in them.

Stately Homes

There is no consortium *per se* of stately homes where the general public may book holidays, but several owners of our British stately homes do, in fact, either accept weekend visitors as their guests (ie, they act as hosts), or hire out their homes for a week or more. Prices are naturally in accordance with the accommodation and prestige being offered.

Since the upkeep costs of stately homes are extremely high, the larger estates are often compelled to think of ways of paying for that upkeep. In many cases, that may mean tours around part of a home. It may mean that an amusement park or recreational area of some kind will be added to the estate to encourage the public to spend money. In other instances, an incentive company will sell a 'guest of a lord' theme to overseas visitors on a commissionable basis. In each of these cases, there is a need for staff to serve tea, to act as informed guides, and to manage the actual property, bearing in mind fishing and hunting rights etc. A training in horticulture could result in a position with a stately home's estate – an end result you might not have anticipated.

A newer development in this country is the introduction of all-year-round, all-weather holiday villages such as Center Parcs. These not only offer good sports and leisure facilities to the holidaymaker, but some also ensure year-round employment possibilities. Perhaps taking the lead from the holiday villages, more and more local authorities are opening entertainment and leisure complexes – a swimming pool is no longer somewhere just to go and swim, it's a place to stay all day, with restaurant and crèche facilities and indoor games areas. For day visitors there are huge theme or leisure parks, some of which also have indoor areas. In many of these complexes there are permanent employment opportunities for any of the following: cleaners, laundry workers, maintenance engineers, joiners, plumbers, caterers, sports coaches, ride attendants, nursery/crèche staff, car park attendants, clerical and administrative staff, booking clerks, pool attendants and so on.

Bed and Breakfast

Frankly, anyone can run a bed and breakfast guest house if they can run a home. If you can make a couple of beds, cook bacon and eggs and dust a living room, you could start your own business. Making that business profitable, however, is another story. Being in the right location has a lot to do with success. Registering with the local tourist board gives authority and support, and publications are available listing accredited bed and breakfast guest houses throughout the country.

Country House Hotels

This term usually refers not only to a rural location but also to a type of operation: small, intimate and with the atmosphere of a private home. These need not be expensive but some, with special emphasis on personal service and style, ask the same rates as large city hotels. Unlike the latter, though, the small country hotels tend to hire young local people for their staff, preferring to train them to their own particular requirements, rather than affording the salary of a management trainee who could be set in a chain hotel mould.

Coach Companies

With over 6,000 coach companies in the UK there are job opportunities for drivers, engineers, operations and administrative staff, guides and tour managers.

In Europe there are many thousands more coach companies, particularly in Germany, France, Italy, Belgium, the Netherlands and Spain. These often employ English-speaking tour managers and drivers as they are contracted by American companies for European tours.

Many coach companies operate their own excursions and tour programmes, both in the UK and on the Continent. As these often specialise in supplying their local markets, the best way to make contact is to look in *Yellow Pages*, ask the local tourist board and look for excursion advertisements in the local papers.

The law says that it is illegal for a driver to guide while his coach is moving, and drivers' hours regulations mean that after driving he can't go on to work as a courier or tour manager, so there will be more and more work for guides and tour managers.

National Express operates a network of scheduled services right across the country to about 1,300 destinations. Many of these journeys are Rapide services, which require a steward/hostess on board to serve drinks and sandwiches. Staff need basic food hygiene training, and are then taught the normal customer service and basic information procedures on short courses held throughout the country. Training in basic emergency or first aid is also useful.

Approach local coach operators for jobs, or major coach stations to find out names of operators who provide Rapide services. Or ask the steward/hostess when you travel on a Rapide coach (they have special rates for students).

Companies are often divided into subsidiaries dealing with different market segments. Besides travel from A to B, there may be tour movement sectors, conference traffic, city sightseeing and maybe an executive hire section when on-board hostesses are in demand.

Courses
The Chartered Institute of Transport can advise on courses for

CPC (Certificate of Professional Competence) which is necessary for coach company traffic managers. There are short courses too: the RSA is the awarding body and can give a list of training providers.

Regional tourist boards offer guide training, as does the Tourism Training Organisation.

Contact St John Ambulance or the Red Cross for first aid training; in Germany coach drivers must have basic first aid training before they can obtain their licence. The Bus and Coach Council can advise on local driver training.

Your local environmental health officer can tell you which colleges offer food hygiene courses, or contact the Association of Couriers in Tourism.

Rail Travel

Working for the railways does not mean only being a train driver, guard or ticket collector. The Railways Board, like the tourist boards and airlines, covers a wide gamut of jobs. It, too, has its planning and research divisions, its conference office, its sales and marketing department, and its press and promotions office. Equally, you could work in reservations and ticketing or even in catering as a cook or a steward.

British Rail has its own management trainee schemes. Candidates can be either graduates or clerical staff. Although the majority of business is naturally associated with transport, British Rail is involved in other fields, such as engineering manufacture, shipping, catering, consultancy, and working with continental railways. The prime asset you could possess for entering management is the ability to communicate with people at all levels. Graduates opting for the passenger business section must have a flair for identifying new opportunities in the travel market and an interest in using analytical and numerate skills to design and develop services. Training for the freight businesses involves the determining of individual needs of industries, manufacturers and distributors; planning the logistics; negotiating the price; making sure the contracts work and pay.

Passenger and freight divisions both come under business management, but there are other career areas, namely operations management, finance/accountancy management, personnel management, engineering management, engineering and scientific research and development, operational research, computer programming, quantity surveying, estate management, and catering management.

To apply for one of the training schemes you should have, or expect to have, an honours degree. Some additional requirements apply to certain schemes, but if you want further information your careers office will put you in touch with the local BritRail contract officer.

Case Study

Gary joined BritRail straight from school and was trained on the spot as a steward.

> You don't need any qualifications but good English is an obvious help, as is appearance – you are, after all, in close contact with passengers. My head steward trained me but there is a restaurant car which has been turned into a special training school, which travels up and down the country. Courses are given on this at the various stops it makes.
>
> I work three days a week though they vary and I never know which train I'll be on or where I'll be going on what is known as my 'spare' day. The rest of the time, I stick to the same route. For me that means four trips a day, taking about 14½ hours – a typical day for most stewards. There are three stewards and one stewardess on my train, all working as a team under a head steward. The trays of food are heavy so you need to be fairly strong, and serving food on a fast-moving train has its problems!
>
> On each of the four trips we serve breakfast, lunch, high tea and dinner. We also lay up and clear away and wash up. I sometimes do special work on exhibition trains or VIP excursions. The perks include tips from customers and also free rail passes and reduced fares.

Channel Tunnel

The opening of the tunnel means that companies using it, such as Eurostar, will need staff, with a high priority given to those applicants speaking French and other European languages.

Chapter 8

Business Travel

What is Business Travel?

The answer is precisely what it says – travel arrangements for anyone visiting a destination in a business capacity as opposed to a holiday one. Hence an airline's 'business class'(though it may use another name such as 'club' or 'ambassador') is geared to a frequent traveller who needs that extra amount of leg room and slightly better service because flying itself is merely part of the day's work. Hence, also, the 'business hotel', which can offer amenities necessary to the guest who may not have scheduled or social hours, such as 24-hour room service, mini bars, same-day valet service etc. Additionally, the business class hotel will automatically have services like telex, electronic mail, fax, secretarial etc and will be able to offer varying sized function rooms for private meetings, conferences or meals.

Business travel may involve an individual or it may involve a group. Work in this segment of the travel industry may mean making the travel arrangements for many executives in a company totally unrelated to travel, or it may mean working in a travel agency specifically dealing with business group travel. It may mean arranging a conference for a company totally unrelated to travel; being a professional conference organiser (PCO) for several different companies; acting as a conference executive at a hotel, tourist board, city council etc; being a sales executive for a conference centre.

Conference Travel

As mentioned above, this is part of the business travel scene as it relates to groups of people attending a meeting in this country or abroad. It is a growing part of the travel industry and well worth career consideration.

Conference Hotels/Venues

From the point of view of a hotel or other venue, a good selling technique is vital. Conference executives must promote their own venue as *the* right one for given groups to bring in the business. They will be expected to know their product thoroughly and sell it only to those for whom it is suitable, if they are hoping for repeat business. They will be expected to negotiate rates that are profitable to their own venue and appropriate to the buyers. Inevitably they will be called on to make sales calls which may mean travelling abroad as well as throughout the UK.

Professional Conference Organiser (PCO)

A PCO generally has to organise a conference or meeting, starting several months or even years ahead to plan the programme, invite the speakers and organise the venue.

During the run-up to the event the PCO will promote the conference, send out literature, take bookings from delegates, liaise with the venue, possibly organise hotel accommodation, book speakers, print conference documents, devise interesting menus, liaise with police, book coaches, arrange a spouse programme, order delegates' kits, organise audiovisual equipment, book temporary staff etc. All this may be organised in-house or subcontracted, but it's the PCO who takes overall responsibility.

Unfortunately, the PCO's job is relatively new, and quite often a company will ask almost any member of staff to arrange its annual meeting, function, sales conference etc, not realising the job is highly skilled. A PCO is someone who may have had experience in the travel industry, worked part time at conferences, or often a secretary who has been asked to run a function for the firm and discovered a hidden talent for organisations.

ACE (Association of Conference Executives) are currently developing a NVQ/SVQs which should mean a more structured and efficient approach to working in this sector. A recent government survey said there are approximately 100,000 people engaged in exhibition, conference and meeting organisation, either full or part-time.

Sometimes the PCO will organise an exhibition to run alongside a conference, or a conference will be part of an exhibition. For business travel clerks, organising visits to trade shows and exhibitions abroad will be an important part of the job.

A conference officer is likely to work for a city or town council 'selling' the place as a whole rather than a particular venue within it. He or she will have thorough knowledge of what is available in the area, for whom and for what numbers it would be suitable and why. Conference enquiries and sometime also booking are handled.

Incentive Travel

Incentive trips are what companies offer their personnel as a reward for increased business. Sales teams are often the target – those selling over and above certain amounts being eligible for the holiday. In order to make employees desirous of doing better to gain the trip, the trip itself has to be of an exciting nature.

There are growing numbers of travel companies specialising entirely in incentive travel arrangements. A recent survey showed over 30 companies with turnovers ranging from £1 million up to £47 million per year. Here again, it is packaging various holiday elements, but generally not on a cut-price basis. An incentive organiser is expected to be creative and imaginative. Theme parties, unusual venues and out-of-the-ordinary things to do become necessities: the right hotel with the same accommodation and treatment for all winners, the right mode of travel to inspire greater work efforts and an itinerary that sounds appealing.

Business Travel Clerk

This job needs someone with an excellent knowledge of geography. When a clients asks for 'a flight to Tirana tomorrow' you have to know where it is, which is the quickest way to get there, what visas and jabs are needed, and which is the best hotel.

Business travel clerks may seldom meet a client face to face as most contacts are made by telephone. The work itself can be highly pressurised too, with companies' representatives and individuals requiring carefully tailored itineraries which are worked out to a strict timetable. One client may need a straight-forward flight booking, while another may be making several flights and train journeys needing accurate connections, plus hotel bookings, hire cars etc, over a period of weeks. Even a single flight booking can involve a choice of maybe 50 differently priced and timed flights with varying facilities. The business travel clerk has to get the client what he or she wants, whether it's economy, comfort or even a particular seat on an aircraft. Details have to be carefully worked out and last-minute changes, of which there are many, dealt with.

Most of the work is done within the travel agent's offices, using fax, phone, telex and computer to receive instructions, make bookings and print tickets, which are then posted or taken by messenger to a company. Paperwork tends to be relegated to the end of the day as the phone takes precedence and dictates the work pace.

Different travel agencies operate their business travel arrangements in different ways. Some concentrate solely on business travel, while other have a section specialising in the business side of things.

Pay rates for business travel clerks tend to be higher than for those selling holiday travel because of the more complex nature of the work and the extra knowledge that is required.

Corporate Hospitality

Corporate hospitality is when a company decided to invite favoured clients or suppliers for a day out, choosing somewhere special such as Derby Day, rugby finals, polo etc, or perhaps arranging a private event at a stately home with balloon ascents, go-karting, hawking and falconry etc, or a day out on the river, a visit to the ballet or some special event.

Catering has to be of the highest standard, as does safety, so there are job opportunities here especially for anyone who likes hard work in a different venue almost every day.

Chapter 9

Public Relations, Press and Promotion Work

In one word, this is communications. Almost every aspect of the travel world has a person or department dealing with the media to publicise and market destination, product, image or event, and there is no guaranteed route to a career in these areas.

The Travel PRO

The travel public relations officer may work in-house for a tour company or for a public relations agency that handles that account. Skills required to become a travel PRO are the same for most other areas of public relations: a talent for writing, as press releases will be part of the job; a flair for organisation to cope with events, promotions and brochure launches that relate to the client; the right likeable attitude for working with other people, particularly those in the media.

Creativity – a flow of ideas – is an important aspect of the job. Knowledge of print, layout and production costs is often helpful. A journalistic background regularly leads to a position in public relations and any course in marketing or communications could well earn you an executive opening.

Courses in both the aforementioned subjects are available from diploma to degree level but, if you want to start young and learn the practical way, take the secretarial route.

Case Studies

Sarah currently works as a travel account executive in a consultant public relations firm. Now in her late 20s, she left school to take a post-A level, two-year bilingual secretarial course.

The language really helped. When I'd completed the course I went off to Paris and was offered a copywriting job with an ad agency. When I returned to England I worked as a personal assistant in a PR consultancy and then, by luck, on a travel magazine.

Sarah agrees that the 'rounded out' experience was what got her a job with her current employer, first as an assistant account executive and now as a senior one. What does her present job comprise?

Running the account on a day-to-day level is a mainstay, by keeping constant liaison with the client and the press. There's a constant need to generate ideas, both for the client's own promotions and the writers' story angles. Naturally there are news and feature releases to be written and press trips to be organised, co-ordinated and often escorted. Functions and press parties have to be set up and the job may call for the ability to negotiate print and art costs.

The salary range for a public relations officer is an exceptionally broad one. At its most senior level it can run to £25,000 pa or, indeed, much much more. At its junior level, it is more likely to be around £9,500 pa.

Eugene, also in her 20s, is a PR agency employee and equally, to get there, she travelled the secretarial way.

I taught myself copy typing but it was my second employer who sent me to secretarial school. I wanted to work in PR but it's really a matter of timing to find – and get – the right vacancy. When I did, I joined a consultancy as a secretary-cum-assistant to a travel account executive which meant I learnt all there was to know on the job. When the account executive left, I had to step in to hold the fort, proved I could do it, and now I'm fully fledged.

Eugene's work is pretty similar to Sarah's but she adds:

The travel PRO may well have to attend several annual conferences as a client representative, hire guest speakers or entertainers for certain functions, assist with audiovisual presentations, come up with giveaway possibilities, and follow through on obtaining and distributing them.

The Travel Writer

There is no set way to become a travel writer. The system which applies to fashion, feature or news writing will similarly apply to the travel field but, because it is considered to be one of the most glamorous areas with some of the best perks, it is also one of the most competitive to break into. When such an opening occurs on a newspaper or magazine, it is often offered to another existing member of staff covering a completely different area. On the other hand, a secretarial position could eventually lead to it as might freelance writing.

If you want to ensure a career in journalism (of any kind), it is best to apply to a local or regional paper for employment as an indentured trainee. If you pass the probationary period, you will be sent on block-release to a college accredited by the National Council for the Training of Journalists (NCTJ). You could also apply direct to the latter for a place on the one-year full-time, pre-entry course, or in some cases receive training on the spot from newspaper groups whose schemes meet the NCTJ requirements.

With natural writing talent and a bit of a pushy streak, you could be lucky enough to omit all this, by beavering away at trying to sell articles until you get one published. If the disappointment of several rejections is too much, a writing career is not for you, but if you study the market for which you wish to write first, can type clean copy to style, either amusing or factual, you stand a chance.

Case Study

Andy (30) did not have training, but he did like to write. After a couple of years getting nowhere, he acquired a freelance contract to write travel for a giveaway magazine. Though it subsequently folded, he is now the travel editor for a prestigious national glossy magazine.

> It took a lot of knocking on doors, futile effort and time and many disappointments. But, finally, I found an editor who liked the way I wrote and I was called in for an interview. Once you have published articles to show, you're on your way to becoming a name, and can apply to join the Chartered Institute of Journalists' Travel Specialists Group.

The Travel Photographer

The British Institute of Professional Photography recognises several courses that are available but, if you have an eye for the visual, a qualification in general photography might start you off. An inherent knack for taking a good picture is the alternative.

Representatives or tour guides keen on photography should

take their cameras; good shots can be offered to their company's brochure planning department and it is customary for shots used to be paid for. **NB** Take out insurance as your camera won't generally be covered on your company's insurance.

Chapter 10
Invest in Yourself

If you are serious about working in the tourism industry, and want to learn as much about it as possible, start networking! Begin by belonging to the appropriate association. Some have special student memberships at lower rates; you have everything except voting rights.

Tourism is a very sociable industry, and members of different sectors usually belong to their own association, which organises visits, meetings and training courses for members where you can gain a 'flavour' of the industry, meet prospective employers and learn lots of valuable information. Regional tourist boards often offer individual membership, and again there are many benefits.

The Tourism Society is an all-embracing group of top tourism professionals, where you can meet people from across a wide spectrum, including some of the more progressive tourism lecturers who like to keep up with what is new.

And do learn a business language. There is a worrying trend for Europeans to come to Britain for training and then stay on and take some of the top jobs, especially in hotels, leaving the junior jobs to the British! Hoteliers say this is because staff in contact with guests have to speak three languages (English plus two others).

What Language?

Think about groups of countries and the common denominator language such as Spanish, which is useful for all the South American nations (except Brazil where Portuguese is spoken). French was *the* diplomatic language and often spoken by the older generation as the sign of a classical education. It's also useful for many ex-French colonies in Africa and the Caribbean.

German was once the language of engineers, and was very influential in central and eastern Europe.

The Russian language was forced on the Eastern bloc countries, and although the younger generation want to speak English, older people had to learn Russian and will use it to communicate between other ex-Communist countries.

The Turkish-speaking Ottoman Empire had tremendous influence throughout the Middle East and Asia. With the southern Russian states emerging along the silk route with oil money in their coffers, this language could be extremely useful as a basis.

Arabic is obviously useful, and the main Chinese dialects of Mandarin and Cantonese are spoken by many Far Eastern visitors.

Japanese visitors may soon outnumber Americans; both the British Tourist Authority and the London Tourist Board encourage people working in tourism to learn this language.

To start with, French, Spanish, German or Italian will probably be the most useful to you, but if you speak an unusual business language your CV might be the one that stands out. But don't count on it.

Chapter 11

Courses and Training

All the associations or companies mentioned below can advise on training. Either phone or send a large sae for details. Addresses are in Chapter 12.

ABTA (Association of British Travel Agents) National Training Board provides lists of colleges and organisations offering NVQs/SVQs – see Chapter 12 for addresses. They also run a College of Open Learning.

ACE (Association of Conference Executives) runs short courses for PCOs and day seminars dealing with legal, insurance, safety and general interest subjects.

Achievement through Training runs courses for unemployed people in Liverpool.

Airlines. Ask the Airline you want to work for, as they carry out their own training for cabin crew.

Bus and Coach Council runs courses for coach operators and drivers.

Business Travel
Association of Conference Executives, see ACE above.
Guild of Business Travel Agents.

Chartered Institute of Transport can suggest where to obtain training to work in transport, coaching and at airports.

Conferences
Association of Conference Executives (see ACE above)
International Association of Professional Congress Organisers.

Corporate Hospitality
Association of Conference Executives (see ACE above)
Corporate Hospitality Association

Guild of Business Travel Agents.

Ecole Hôtelier de Lausanne, see page 9.

EFAH (European Foundation for the Accreditation of Hotel School Programmes) will advise on accredited schools.

Farm Tourism, National Trust, Parks etc
Council for National Parks
Farm Holiday Bureau
Institute of Leisure and Amenity Management
National Trust.

Guides
Ask local tourist board for details of courses
Sight and Sound Distance Learning
Tourism Training Organisation.

HCIMA (Hotel, Catering and Institutional Management Association) and **Hotel and Catering Training Company** will supply lists of organisations and colleges offering training.

Hotels
Ecole Hôtelier de Lausanne
EFAH
HCIMA
Hotel and Catering Training Company
Swiss National Tourist Office.

Languages
National Business Language Information Service.
For courses abroad: UK office of embassy or cultural institute of appropriate country.
    If English is *not* your mother tongue there is TEP (Tourism English Proficiency), and Oxford exam offered in colleges around the world.

Meet-and-Greet Staff
ABTA
Local Tourist Board Guide training
Sight and Sound Distance Learning
Tourism Training Organisation.

Museums
Association of Independent Museums
Museums Association.

Representatives (Reps)
ABTA and ABTA Distance Learning
Achievement through Training
Tourism Training Organisation.

Restaurants
The Restaurateurs' Association says at the moment there is no complete list of approved catering colleges. Try talking to good chefs at local restaurants, Springboard in London, and the Hotel and Catering Training Company.

Sight and Sound have a Distance Learning (home study) course suitable for basic training for guides, representatives and coach stewards and hostesses.

Swiss National Tourist Office can supply a list of hotel and catering schools in Switzerland.

Tour Operators
ABTA National Training Board
British Incoming Tour Operators Association.

Tourism
English Heritage
Local Tourist Boards.
For degrees and specialised courses, the Tourism Society published *Profile of Tourism Studies and Degrees Courses in the UK*, cost £5.

Tourism Society runs evening seminars on subjects of interest to members.

Tourism Training Organisation runs courses for coach tour guides, representatives, meet-and-greet staff, conference and exhibition receptionists.

Training Academy runs courses for unemployed people.

Transport
Bus and Coach Council
Chartered Institute of Transport.

Travel Agents
ABTA National Training Board.

University of Oxford Delegacy of Local Examinations offers an exam in Tourism English Proficiency (TEP) for those whose mother tongue is *not* English, and want to be assessed at speaking idiomatic English for the tourism industry.

Chapter 12

Useful Addresses

Some associations have only a part-time staff and therefore prefer you to phone.

ABTA National Training Board, Barratt House, 11–17 Chertsey Road, Woking, Surrey GU21 5AL; 0486 227321 (enclose a large sae)

Achievement through Training, 87 Lord Street, Liverpool L2 6PG

Association of Conference Executives, Riverside House, High Street, Huntingdon, Cambridgeshire PE18 6SG; 0480 457595

Association of Couriers in Tourism, 41 Fitzwilliam Street, Swinton, Rotherham, Yorkshire; 0709 586927

Association of Graduate Careers Advisory Services, Central Services Unit, Crawford House, Precinct Centre, Oxford Road, Manchester M13 9EP; 061-273 4233

Association of Independent Museums, PO Box 68, Chalon Way, St Helens WA9 1LL; 0744 22766

Association of Pleasure Craft Operators, 35a High Street, Newport, Shropshire TF10 8JW

Association of Professional Tourist Guides, Wessex House, 520 London Road, Mitcham, Surrey CR4 4YQ

Association of Tour Managers, 397 Walworth Road, London SE17 2AW

British Airports Authority plc, Masefield House, Gatwick, West Sussex RH6 0HZ; 0293 517755

British Airways Recruitment and Selection, Meadowbank, PO Box 59, Heathrow Airport, Hounslow, Middlesex

British Association of Leisure Parks, Piers and Attractions, 25 King's Terrace, London NW1 0JP; 071-383 7942

British Association of Tourism Officers, c/o Plymouth Marketing Bureau, St Andrews Street, Plymouth, Devon PL1 2AH; 0752 261125

British Federation of Hotel, Guest House and Self-Catering Associations, 5 Sandicroft Road, Blackpool, Lancashire FY1 2RY; 0253 52683

British Holiday and Home Parks Association, Chichester House, 31 Park Road, Gloucester GL1 1LH

British Incoming Tour Operators Association, 120 Wilton Road, London SW1V 1JZ; 071-931 0601

British Institute of Professional Photography, Fox Talbot House, Amwell End, Ware, Hertfordshire SG12 9HN; 0920 464011

British Tourist Authority, Thames Tower, Blacks Road, London W6 9EL; 081-846 9000

Bus and Coach Council, Sardinia House, Lincoln's Inn Fields, London WC2A 3LZ who run:

Bus and Coach Training, 40 High Street, Rickmansworth, Hertfordshire WD3 1ER; 0923 896607

Business and Technology Education Council, Central House, Upper Woburn Place, London WC1H 0HH; 071-413 8400

Chartered Institute of Journalists, 2 Dock Offices, Surrey Quays Road, London SE16 2XL; 071-252 1187

Chartered Institute of Transport, 80 Portland Place, London W1N 4DP; 071-636 9952

CILT (Centre for Information on Language Teaching and Research) 20 Bedfordbury, London WC2N 4LB; 071-379 5134

City and Guilds of London Institute, 76 Portland Place, London W1N 4AA; 071-278 2468

Civil Aviation Authority, CAA House, 45-59 Kingsway, London WC2B 6TE; 071-379 7311

Corporate Hospitality Association, 0737 833963. Telephone enquiries only.

Council for National Parks, 246 Lavender Hill, London SW11 1LJ; 071-924 4077

Countryside Commission, Publications Despatch Department, 19 Albert Road, Manchester M19 2EQ; 061-224 6287

Ecole Hôtelier de Lausanne, Le-Chalet-a-Gobet, CH-1000 Lausanne, Switzerland; 21 705 11 11; Fax 21 784 14 07

EFAH (European Foundation for the Accreditation of Hotel School Programmes), c/o HOTREC 111 Boulevard Anspach, BTE4, 1000 Brussels; 32 2513 6323; Fax 32 2502 4173

English Heritage, 14 Clifford Street, London W1X 1RB; 071-973 3862

English Nature, Northminster House, Peterborough, Cambridgeshire PE1 1UA; 0733 40345

. English Tourist Board, Thames Tower, Blacks Road, London W6 9EL; 081-846 9000

Farm Holiday Bureau, NAC Stoneleigh, Warwickshire; 0203 696909

Guild of Business Travel Agents, 3 Premier House, 10 Greycoat Place, London SW1P 1SB; 071-222 2744

Guild of Guide Lecturers, The Guild House, 52D Borough High Street, London SE1 1XN; 071-403 1115

Hotel and Catering Training Company, International House, High Street, Ealing, London W5 5DB; 081-579 2400

Hotel Catering and Institutional Management Association, 191 Trinity Road, London SW17 7HN; 081-672 4251

Institute of Baths and Recreational Management, 36-38 Sherrard Street, Melton Mowbray, Leicestershire LE13 1XJ; 0664 65531

Institute of Leisure and Amenity Management, Lower Basildon, Reading, Berkshire RG8 9NE; 0491 874222

Institute of Travel and Tourism, 113 Victoria Street, St Albans, Hertfordshire AL1 3TJ; 0727 854395

International Association of Professional Congress Organisors, 40 rue Washington, B-1050 Brussels, Belgium; (32) 2-640 18 08; Fax +32 2-646 05 25

Local Government Management Board, Arndale House, The Arndale Centre, Luton, Bedfordshire LU1 2TS; 0582 451166

► London Tourist Board, 26 Grosvenor Gardens, London SW1V 0DV; 071-730 3450

Museums Association, 42 Clerkenwell Close, London EC1R 0PA; 071-608 2933

National Business Language Information Service; 071-379 5131. Telephone enquiries only.

National Council for the Training of Journalists, Carlton House, Hemnall Street, Epping, Essex CM16 4NL; 0378 72395

National Council for Vocational Qualifications, 222 Euston Road, London NW1 2BZ; 071-387 9898

National Sea Training College, Denton, Gravesend, Kent DA12 2HR; 0474 363656

National Trust, 36 Queen Anne's Gate, London SW1H 9AS; 071-222 9251

National Trust Scotland, 5 Charlotte Square, Edinburgh EH2 4DU; 031-226 5922

Northern Ireland Tourist Board, River House, 48 High Street, Belfast BT1 2DS

Recreation Managers Association, 5 Balfour Road, Weybridge, Surrey KT13 8HE

Restaurateurs' Association of Great Britain, 190 Queens Gate, London SW7 5EU

Royal Society of Arts Examinations Board (RSA), Westwood Way, Coventry CV4 8HS; 0203 470033

Scottish Tourist Board, 23 Ravelston Terrace, Edinburgh EH4 3EU

Scottish Vocational Education Council, Hanover House, 24 Douglas Street, Glasgow G2 7NQ; 041-248 7900

Sight and Sound Distance Learning, Quill Mill, Banbury, Oxfordshire; better to telephone on 071-351 4434

Springboard, 1 Denmark Street, London WC2H 8LP (for information on recruitment and training programmes in travel, tourism, leisure, hotel and catering in London); 071-497 8654

Swiss National Tourist Office, Swiss Centre, New Coventry Street, London W1V 8EE; 071-734 1921

Tourism Society, 26 Chapter Street, London SW1P 4ND; 071-834 0461. This is an association for members and information on courses in the industry, *not* a general enquiry point for the tourism industry.

Tourism Training Organisation, 54 Ifield Road, London SW10 9AD; 071-351 4434

Training Academy, 23 Newman Street, London W1P 3HA; 071-636 5454

University of Oxford Delegacy of Local Examinations, Ewert House, Ewert Place, Summertown, Oxford OX2 7BZ

Wales Tourist Board, Brunel House, 2 Fitzalan Road, Cardiff CF2 1UY; 0222 499909

Regional Tourist Boards

Cumbria Tourist Board, Ashleigh, Holly Road, Windermere, Cumbria LA23 2AQ

East Anglia Tourist Board, Toppesfield Hall, Hadleigh, Suffolk IP7 5DN

East Midlands Tourist Board, Exchequergate, Lincoln LN2 1PZ

Heart of England Tourist Board, Woodside, Larkhill Road, Worcester WR5 2EF

London Tourist Board and Convention Bureau, 26 Grosvenor Gardens, London SW1W 0DU

Northumbria Tourist Board, Aykley Heads, Durham City, Durham DH1 5UX

North West Tourist Board, Swan House, Swan Meadow Road, Wigan Pier, Lancashire WN3 5BB

South East England Tourist Board, The Old Brew House, Warwick Park, Tunbridge Wells, Kent TN2 5TU

Southern Tourist Board, 40 Chamberlayne Road, Eastleigh, Hampshire SO5 5JH

West Country Tourist Board, 60 St David's Hill, Exeter, Devon EX4 4SY

Yorkshire and Humberside Tourist Board, 312 Tadcaster Road, York YO2 2HF

Accredited Organisations

The following list of colleges is approved by ABTA to run courses in and to assess National and Scottish Vocational Qualifications pertaining to travel services.

FE = Further Education

National

ABTA College of Open Learning, Woking, Surrey; 0483 727321

London

City of Westminster College, 25 Paddington Green, London, W2 1NB; 071-723 8826

Hendon College of FE, Colindale, London NW9 5RA; 081-200 8300

London College of Printing and Distributive Trades, London WC2H 7LE; 071-735 8484

Southwark College, The Cut, London, SE1 8LE; 071-928 9561

Westminster College, Battersea Park Road, London SW11 4JR; 071-720 2121

South East

Amersham & Wycombe College, Amersham, Buckinghamshire HP7 9HN; 0494 721121

Aylesbury College, Aylesbury, Buckinghamshire HP21 8PD; 0296 434111

Bexley College (Formerly Erith), Belvedere, Kent DA17 6JA; 0322 442331

Brooklands College, Weybridge, Surrey KT13 8TT; 0932 853300

Canterbury College of Technology, Canterbury, Kent CT1 3AJ; 0227 766081

Carshalton College of FE, Carshalton, Surrey SM5 2EJ; 081-770 6800

Croydon College Selhurst, Croydon, Surrey CR9 2LY; 081-684 9266

East Berkshire College at Langley, Maidenhead, Berkshire SL3 8BY; 0628 25221

Eastbourne College of Arts and Technology, East Sussex BN21 2HS; 0323 644711

East Surrey College, Redhill, Surrey RH1 2JX; 0737 772611

Enfield College, Enfield, Middlesex EN3 5HA; 081-443 3434

Farnborough College of Technology, Farnborough, Surrey GU14 6SB; 0252 515511

Guildford College of Technology, Guildford, Surrey GU1 1EZ; 0483 31251

Harlow College, Harlow, Essex CM20 1LT; 0279 441288

Hertford Regional College (Ware Centre), Hertfordshire SG12 9JF; 0920 465441

Highbury College of Technology, Portsmouth, Hampshire PO6 2SA; 0705 383131

Newbury College, Newbury, Berkshire RG13 1PQ; 0635 37000

Northbrook College of Design and Technology, Worthing, Sussex BN12 6NV; 0903 830057

North West Kent College of Technology, Dartford, Kent DA1 2LU; 0322 275517

Oaklands College, Welwyn Garden City, Hertfordshire AL8 6AH; 0707 326318

Oxford College of FE, Oxford OX1 1SA; 0865 245871

Queen Elizabeth Training College, Leatherhead, Surrey KT22 0BN; 037 284 2204

Thurrock College, Aveley, South Ockenden, Essex RM15 4HT; 0708 863011

West Kent College, Tonbridge, Kent TN9 2PW; 0732 358101

South West

East Devon College of FE, Tiverton, Devon EX16 6SH; 0884 254247

Evesham College of FE, Evesham, Worcestershire WR11 6LP; 0386 41091

Gloucestershire College of Art and Technology, Cheltenham GL50 2RR; 0242 532048

Herefordshire College of Technology, Hereford HR1 1LS; 0432 352235

North Devon College, Barnstaple, North Devon EX31 2BQ; 0271 45291

Plymouth College of FE, Devonport, Plymouth PL1 5QG; 0752 382000

St Austell College, (formerly Mid-Cornwall), Cornwall PL25 4BW; 0726 67911

Somerset College of Arts and Technology, Taunton TA1 5AX; 0823 283403

Soundwell College, Bristol BS16 4RL; 0272 675101

Midlands

Birmingham College of Food, Summer Row, Birmingham B3 1JB; 021-235 3761

Broxtowe College of FE, Chilwell, Nottingham NG9 4AH; 0602 228161

Henley College of FE, Coventry, West Midlands, CV2 1ED; 0203 611021

High Peak College of FE, Buxton, Derbyshire SK17 9JZ; 0298 71100

Kingsthorpe Upper School, Northampton; 0604 716106

Loughborough College, Leicestershire LE11 3BT; 0509 215831

North East Worcestershire College, Bromsgrove B60 1PQ; 0527 570020

North Nottinghamshire College of FE, Worksop S81 7HP; 0909 473561

Sandwell College, West Midlands B70 8DW; 021-556 6000

Solihull College of Technology, Solihull, Birmingham B91 1SB; 021-711 2111

Stoke-on-Trent College, Staffordshire ST4 2DG; 0782 202561

Stratford-upon-Avon College, Warwickshire CV37 9QR; 0789 266245

Tresham College, Kettering, Northamptonshire NN15 7BS; 0536 410252

Eastern Region

Braintree College of FE, Braintree, Essex CM7 5SN; 0376 21711

Lowestoft College, Suffolk NR32 2NB; 0502 583521

Norfolk College of Arts and Technology, Kings Lynn PE30 2QW; 0553 761144

Norwich City College, Norwich, Norfolk NR2 2LJ; 0603 660011

Peterborough Regional College, Peterborough, Cambridgeshire PE1 4DZ; 0733 67366

South East Essex College of Art and Technology, Southend-on-Sea SS2 6LS; 0702 220400

North East

Barnsley College, Barnsley, South Yorkshire S70 2AX; 0226 730191

Cleveland College of FE, Redcar, Cleveland TS10 1EZ; 0642 473132

Grantham College of FE, Grantham, Lincolnshire NG31 9AP; 0476 63141

Hull College of FE, Hull HU1 3DG; 0482 29943

Kirby College of FE, Middlesbrough TS5 5PT; 0642 813706

New College Durham, Durham DH1 5ES; 091-386 2421

North Lindsey College of Technology, Scunthorpe, Humberside DN17 1AJ; 0724 281111

North Tyneside College, Wallsend, Tyne & Wear NE28 9NJ; 091-262 4081

Park Lane College of FE, Leeds LS3 1AA; 0532 443011

Rockingham College of FE, Rotherham S63 6PX; 0709 760310

Wakefield District College, West Yorkshire WE1 2DH; 0924 370501

York College of Arts and Technology, York YO2 1UA; 0904 704141

North West

Blackpool and The Fylde College, Bispham, Blackpool FY2 0HB; 0253 52352

Bolton Metropolitan College, Bolton, Lancashire BL2 1ER; 0204 31411

Bury Metropolitan College of FE, Bury, Lancashire M25 5NH; 061-763 1505

Carlisle College, Carlisle, Cumbria CA1 1HS; 0228 24464

City of Liverpool Community College, Liverpool L1 4DB; 051-259 1124

Hopwood Hall College, Middleton, Manchester OL12 6RY; 061-643 7560

Macclesfield College of FE, Cheshire SK11 8LF; 0625 27744

Preston College, Fulwood, Preston, Lancashire PR2 4UR; 0772 716511

St Helens Community College, Merseyside WA10 1PZ; 0744 33766

Salford College of FE, Worsley, Manchester M28 4QD; 061-702 8272

South Cheshire College, Crewe CW2 8AB; 0270 69133

South Trafford College, West Timperley, Altrincham WA14 5PQ; 061-973 7064

Southport College, Southport, Lancashire PR9 0TT; 0704 5424111

Stockport College of Further and Higher Education, Stockport SK1 3UQ; 061-480 7331

Wigan and Leigh College, Wigan WN1 1RS; 0942 494911

Wales

Barry College, Barry Island CF6 8YJ; 0446 743519

Swansea College, Tycoch Road, Sketty, Swansea SA2 9EB; 0792 206871

Scotland

Aberdeen College of FE, Bridge of Don, Aberdeen AB2 8DB; 0224 640366

Dundee College of FE, Dundee DD3 8LE; 0382 29151

Glasgow College of Food Technology, Glasgow G1 2TG; 041-552 3751

Motherwell College, Lanarkshire ML1 2DD; 0698 259641

Northern Ireland

Belfast Institute of Further and Higher Education, Ravenhill Road, Belfast BT2 7GX; 0232 457008

North Down and Ards College of FE, Bangor, Co Down BT20 4TF; 0247 271254

Islands

Highlands College, St Saviour, Jersey JE4 9QA, Channel Islands; 0534 718000

Isle of Man College of FE, Douglas, Isle of Man; 0624 623113

Chapter 13
Useful Publications

General information on jobs and training in travel, tourism, leisure, and catering and hotel management can be found in the following publications:

Careers in Catering and Hotel Management, Kogan Page
Careers in Marketing, Advertising and Public Relations, Kogan Page
Finding a Job...in the USA, Australia, Far East, South Africa etc, Island Publishing
Occupations, COIC
Working in Airports, COIC
Working in the Hospitality Industry, COIC
Working in Leisure, COIC
Working in Ski Resorts, Victoria Pybus, Vacation Work Publications
Working in Travel and Tourism, case studies and some useful job contacts, Island Publishing (0273 440220)

Directories of Further or Higher Education Courses

Compendium of Advanced Courses in Colleges of Further and Higher Education, Regional Advisory Councils
University Entrance: The Official Guide, Association of University Vice-Chancellors and Principals
UCAS Handbook, UCAS
Directory of Further Education (in particular information on courses awarded by City and Guilds, BTEC and SCOTVEC), CRAC

Useful Journals

The following journals advertise job vacancies for the travel and holiday industry, and are available for reference in many public libraries:

Caterer and Hotelkeeper
Overseas Jobs Express
Travel Trade Gazette
Travel Weekly